CUB TALES
&
TRIVIA

CUB TALES
&
TRIVIA

by Fred T. Smith

A&M
Altwerger and Mandel Publishing Company
West Bloomfield, Michigan

Published by
A&M
Altwerger & Mandel Pub. Co., Inc.
6346 Orchard Lake Road, Suite 201
West Bloomfield, Michigan 48322

ISBN 1-878005-05-7

First Edition 1991

Designed by Mary Primeau

CONTENTS

INTRODUCTION
THE GAME FOR ALL AMERICA

by Ernie Harwell

Baseball is President Eisenhower tossing out the first ball of the season, and a pudgy schoolboy playing catch with his dad on a Mississippi farm.

It's the big league pitcher who sings in night clubs, and the Hollywood singer who pitches to the Giants in spring training.

A tall, thin old man waving a scorecard from his dugout — that's baseball. So is the big, fat guy with a bulbous nose running out one of his 714 home runs with mincing steps.

It's America, this baseball. A re-issued newsreel of boyhood dreams. Dreams lost somewhere between boy and man. It's the Bronx cheer and the Baltimore farewell. The left field screen in Boston, the right field dump at Nashville's Sulphur Dell, the open stands in San Francisco, the dusty, wind-swept diamond at Albuquerque. And a rock home plate and a chicken wire backstop — anywhere.

There's a man in Mobile who remembers a triple he saw Honus Wagner hit in Pittsburgh 46 years ago. That's baseball. So is the scout reporting that a 16-year-old sandlot pitcher in Cheyenne is the new "Walter Johnson."

It's a wizened little man shouting insults from the safety of his

1

bleacher seat. And a big, smiling first baseman playfully tousling the hair of a youngster outside the players' gate.

Baseball is a spirited race of man against man, reflex against reflex. A game of inches. Every skill is measured. Every heroic, every failing is seen and cheered — or booed. And then becomes a statistic.

In baseball, democracy shines its clearest. Here the only race that matters is the race to the bag. The creed is the rule book. Color is something to distinguish one team's uniform from another.

Baseball is Sir Alexander Fleming, discoverer of penicillin, asking his Brooklyn hosts to explain Dodger signals. It's player Moe Berg speaking seven languages and working crossword puzzles in Sanskrit. It's a scramble in the box seats for a foul — and a $125 suit ruined. A man barking into a hot microphone about a cool beer, that's baseball. So is the sports writer telling a .383 hitter how to stride, and a 20-victory pitcher trying to write his impressions of the World Series.

Baseball is a ballet without music. Drama without words. A carnival without kewpie dolls.

A housewife in California couldn't tell you the color of her husband's eyes, but she knows that Yogi Berra is hitting .337, has brown eyes, and used to love to eat bananas with mustard. That's baseball. So is the bright sanctity of Cooperstown's Hall of Fame. And the former big leaguer, who is playing out the string in a Class B loop.

Baseball is continuity. Pitch to pitch. Inning to inning. Game to game. Series to series. Season to season.

It's rain, rain, rain splattering on a puddled tarpaulin as thousands sit in damp disappointment. And the click of typewriters and telegraph keys in the press box — like so many awakened crickets. Baseball is a cocky batboy. A lady celebrating a home team rally by mauling her husband with a rolled-up scorecard.

Baseball is the cool, clear eyes of Rogers Hornsby, the flashing spikes of Ty Cobb, an overaged pixie named Rabbit Maranville, and Jackie Robinson testifying before a Congressional hearing.

Baseball? It's just a game — as simple as a ball and a bat, yet, as complex as the American spirit it symbolizes. It's a sport, a business—and sometimes even a religion.

Baseball is Tradition in flannel knickerbockers. And Chagrin in being picked off base. It is Dignity in the blue serge of an umpire running the game by rule of thumb. It is Humor, holding its sides when an errant puppy eludes two groundskeepers and the fastest outfielder. And Pathos, dragging itself off field after being knocked from the box.

Nicknames are baseball. Names like Zeke and Pie and Kiki and Home Run and Cracker and Dizzy and Dazzy.

Baseball is a sweaty, steaming dressing room where hopes and feelings are as naked as the men themselves. It's a dugout with spike-scarred flooring. And shadows across an empty ball park. It's the endless list of names in box scores, abbreviated almost beyond recognition.

The holdout is baseball, too. He wants 55 grand or he won't turn a muscle. But, it's also the youngster who hitchhikes from South Dakota to Florida just for a tryout.

Arguments, "Casey at the Bat", old cigarette cards, photographs, "Take Me Out to the Ball Game"—all of them are baseball.

Baseball is a rookie—his experience no bigger than the lump in his throat—trying to begin fulfillment of a dream. It's a veteran, too—a tired old man of 35, hoping his aching muscles can drag him through another sweltering August and September.

For nine innings, baseball is the story of David and Goliath, of Samson, Cinderella, Paul Bunyan, Homer's *Iliad*, and the *Count of Monte Cristo*.

Willie Mays making a brilliant World Series catch, and then going home to Harlem to play stick-ball in the street with his teen-age pals—that's baseball. So is the husky voice of a doomed Lou Gehrig saying, "I'm the luckiest guy in the world."

Baseball is cigar smoke, hot-roasted peanuts, *The Sporting News*, winter trades, "Down in front," and the Seventh Inning Stretch. Sore arms, broken bats, a no-hitter, and the strains of the *Star-Spangled Banner*.

Baseball is a highly-paid Brooklyn catcher telling the nation's business leaders: "You have to be a man to be a big leaguer, but you have to have a lot of little boy in you, too."

This is a game for America, this baseball!

A game for boys and men.

PART ONE

CHAPTER ONE
THE CHICAGO CUBS:
THE EARLY YEARS 1884–1949

Q   Who managed the Chicago Cubs in 1902, 1903, 1904 and 1905?
A   Frank Selee

Q   Who managed the Cubs from 1905 through 1912?
A   Frank Chance

Q   Who managed the Cubs in 1913?
A   Johnny Evers

Q   Who managed the Cubs in 1914?
A   Hank O'Day managed the club in 1914.

Q   Who managed the Cubs in 1915?
A   Roger Bresnahan

Q   Who managed the Cubs in 1916?
A   Joe Tinker

Q   Who managed the Cubs in 1917 through 1920?
A   Fred Mitchell

Q   Who was the Cubs manager in 1921?
A   John Evers started the season and Bill Killefer finished it. Killefer also managed in 1922, 1923, 1924, and part of 1925.

Q   Who relieved Bill Killefer as manager of the Cubs in 1925?
A   "Rabbit" Maranville

Q   The Cubs had three managers in 1925. Who was the third one?
A   George Gibson

Q   Who relieved Joe McCarthy as manager of the Cubs in 1930?
A   Rogers Hornsby, who managed the rest of 1930, 1931, and part of 1932.

Q   Who relieved Rogers Hornsby as manager in 1932?
A   Charlie Grimm

Q   How long did Grimm manage the Cubs?
A   Grimm managed the Cubs on three different occasions. The first from 1932 to 1938, and then from 1944 to 1949, and again in 1960.

Q   What was Riggs Stephenson's lifetime batting average?
A   .336

Q   What was Riggs Stephenson mainly noted for?
A   He was one of the greatest clutch hitters of all time.

Q   Did Riggs Stephenson ever play in a World Series?
A   Yes, in 1929 and 1932. He went to bat 37 times and got 14 hits for a .378 batting average.

Q   What was Johnny Schmitz's nickname?
A   "Beartracks"

Q   How long did Johnny Schmitz pitch for the Cubs?
A   From 1941 until 1951.

Q   What was Johnny Schmitz's best year?
A   He won 18 and lost 13 in 1948.

Q   Johnny Schmitz was traded to Brooklyn in 1951 along with Rube Walker, Andy Pafko, and Wayne Terwilliger. Whom did the Cubs receive in exchange?
A   Bruce Edwards, Gene Hermanski, Eddie Miksis, and Joe Hatten.

Q   In what year did the Cubs move into Weeghman Park?
A   1916

Q   Ed Reulbach pitched both games of a double-header in 1908. What was outstanding about them?
A   They were both shutouts, beating the Dodgers 5–0 and 3–0.

Q   In what year did the Cubs officially adopt the nickname of their team as the "Cubs"?
A   1907

Q   What is Harry Steinfeldt best known for?
A   Probably as the answer to the great trivia question, "Who was the third baseman in the Tinkers to Chance to Evers infield?"

Q   When did Harry Steinfeldt play for the Cubs?
A   1906 through 1910

Q   Did "Dizzy" Dean ever play for the Cubs?
A   Yes. He came to the Cubs in 1938.

Q   How did the Cubs get "Dizzy" Dean?
A   He came in a trade in April of 1938 in exchange for Curt Davis, Clyde Shoon, and Tuck Stainback and approximately $185,000.00.

Q   How long did "Dizzy" Dean pitch for the Cubs?
A   For parts of four seasons. He was with them from 1938 to 1941.

9

Q   Who was Hugh Duffy?

A   Duffy was an outfielder with Chicago in the National League in 1888 and 1889. He is most noted for the fact that he hit .438 in 1894 when playing with Boston in the National League, the highest batting average of all time.

Q   Did Jimmy Foxx ever play for the Cubs?

A   Yes. He came to the Cubs in 1942 and played there in 1942 and 1944.

Q   What is Jimmy Foxx best remembered for?

A   He hit 58 homeruns in 1932 when he played for the Philadelphia Athletics.

Q   What year was the first Chicago Cub game telecast?

A   It was in a game with the Chicago White Sox, who beat the Cubs 4–1 in 1948 on WGN-TV with Jack Brickhouse as the announcer.

Q   How many times did Rogers Hornsby lead the National League in batting?

A   Seven times

Q   Did Rogers Hornsby ever lead the league in batting when he played for the Cubs?

A   No. He led the league six times when he played with St. Louis and once with the Boston Braves.

Q   What was Andy Pafko's nickname?

A   "Handy" Andy

Q   When did Andy Pafko play for the Cubs?

A   He joined the Cubs in 1943 and stayed with them until he went to Brooklyn in 1951.

Q   How many years did Andy Pafko play in the majors?

A   17 years

Q   What was Andy Pafko's lifetime batting average within five points?
A   .285

Q   Did Andy Pafko ever play in the World Series for the Cubs?
A   Yes, in 1945.

Q   In 1907 the Chicago Cubs pitching staff won 107 games with a team earned run average of 1.73. How many shutouts did they pitch?
A   Thirty-two. Needless to say, they won the pennant that season.

Q   Bruce Sutter was in the National League 11 years. Did he ever start a game?
A   No. He was in 623 ballgames and always in relief.

Q   What was Lon Warneke's nickname?
A   "The Arkansas Hummingbird"

Q   How long did Lon Warneke pitch for the Cubs?
A   Ten years, from 1930 through 1936 and 1942, 1943, and 1945.

Q   How many times did Lon Warneke win 20 or more ballgames?
A   Three times. In 1932 he won 22, in 1934 he won 22, and in 1935 he won 20.

Q   What was Lon Warneke's hometown?
A   Mt. Ida, Arkansas.

Q   Did Lon Warneke win 200 ballgames during his 15-year career?
A   No. He won 193.

11

Q   Was Lon Warneke ever in a World Series for the Cubs?
A   Yes. In 1932 he lost one game. In 1935 he won two and lost none.

Q   Lon Warneke was traded to the Cardinals in 1936. Whom did the Cubs receive in exchange?
A   Rip Collins and Roy Parmalee

Q   Lon Warneke was with the Cubs on two occasions. When did he come back?
A   The Cubs bought him from the Cardinals in the middle of 1942.

Q   An ex-Cub is the only player to play in the World Series for teams from both leagues under the same manager. Who was he?
A   Pat Malone was with the Chicago Cubs in the 1929 Series and pitched for the New York Yankees under Joe McCarthy again in the 1936 Series.

Q   There were two unassisted triple plays made in the big leagues in May 1926. A shortstop for the Cubs made one of them. Who was he?
A   Jimmy Cooney of the Cubs had an unassisted triple play in a game against Pittsburgh. Johnny Neun of Detroit also had an unassisted triple play the next day on May 31, 1926.

Q   What was rather unusual about Hack Wilson hitting 56 homeruns in 1930 and driving in 190 runs?
A   He didn't hit a grand slam all year.

Q   Which National League team was the first team to draw over 1,000,000 fans in one year?
A   The Chicago Cubs drew 1,159,168 people into the ballpark in 1927.

Q   Billy Herman played second base for the Cubs from 1931 to mid-1941. Who took his place?

A   Lou Stringer played most of the season in 1941 after Herman had been traded.

Q   What high school did Phil Cavarretta go to?

A   Phil came out of Lane Tech High School in Chicago as an 18-year-old and played a few games with the Cubs in 1934. He continued to play with the Cubs through 1953, finishing his major league career as a player in 1954 and 1955 with the Chicago White Sox. He managed the Cubs in 1951, 1952, and 1953.

Q   On May 30, 1922 the Chicago Cubs made a trade with the St. Louis Cardinals. What was unusual about it?

A   In the first game of a double-header that day, Max Flack played right field for the Cubs; he then played right field for the Cards in the second game. Cliff Heathcoat played right for the Cardinals in the first game and right for the Cubs in the second game.

Q   What year did the National League first authorize numbering of the players?

A   1931. The American League had started in 1930 with the Yankees numbering the players, and all clubs did it in 1931.

Q   What is the highest batting average for lifetime by a major league baseball player?

A   Ty Cobb hit .367 in his 24-year career in the major leagues, and Rogers Hornsby hit .358 in his 23-year career in the majors. Hornsby played parts of four seasons with the Cubs.

Q   What is the Cub record for most runs batted in one game by an individual player?

A   Heinie Zimmerman drove in nine runs on June 11, 1911.

Q   In how many consecutive games did Billy Williams play?

A   1,117, from 1961 to 1974.

Q   What Cub pitcher appeared in most games?
A   Charlie Root had 201 wins in his 16-year career with the Cubs.

Q   Who was the manager who managed the most years for the Cubs in the modern era?
A   Charlie Grimm managed parts of 14 seasons for the Cubs.

Q   What former Cub pitcher gave up the last homeruns of Babe Ruth's big league career?
A   On May 25, 1935, Ruth hit three homeruns in a game playing for the Boston Braves against the Pittsburgh Pirates. He hit the first one off Red Lucas and the second and third off Guy Bush, a former Cub.

Q   When did Billy Herman play for the Cubs?
A   From 1931 to the middle of 1941.

Q   When Billy Herman left the Cubs, where did he go?
A   He was traded to Brooklyn

Q   Who was Billy Herman traded for?
A   Billy Herman was traded to Brooklyn for Johnny Hudson, Carlie Gilbert, and a lot of cash.

Q   What was Billy Herman's lifetime batting average within five points?
A   .304

Q   Did Billy Herman ever play in the World Series?
A   Yes. He played with the Cubs in 1932, 1935, 1938, and in 1941 with Brooklyn.

Q   What year did Billy Herman go into the Hall of Fame?
A   Billy Herman was inducted into the Hall of Fame in 1975.

14

Q How many years did Billy Herman play in the major leagues?

A He played 15 years in the National League.

Q Did Rogers Hornsby ever play for the Chicago Cubs?

A Yes. He played with the Cubs in 1929, 1930, 1931, and 1932.

Q Within five points, what was Rogers Hornsby's lifetime batting average?

A .358

Q How many years did Rogers Hornsby play in the big leagues?

A 23 years

Q How did the Cubs obtain Ferguson Jenkins?

A The Cubs traded Adolfo Phillips, Jenkins, and John Herrnstein for Larry Jackson and Bob Buhl in 1966.

Q In 1976 two idiots tried to set afire the United States flag in the outfield at Dodger Stadium. Who was the Cub outfielder who rescued the flag?

A Rick Monday

Q When did Lou Boudreau succeed Charlie Grimm as Cub manager?

A In 1960. Boudreau had been announcing the games on the radio and Grimm was managing the Cubs. They replaced each other on May 4, 1960.

Q In May of 1942 a Boston Braves pitcher hit three homeruns to help defeat the Cubs at Wrigley Field. Who was the Braves pitcher?

A Jim Tobin

Q Whom did Stan Musial, the great Cardinal outfielder, get his 3,000th hit off?

A Moe Drabowsky, then with the Cubs. The stadium was Wrigley Field.

Q   Who was Joe Tinker?
A   Joe Tinker was the shortstop in the Cubs' famous double-play combination, Tinkers to Evers to Chance.

Q   When did Tinker start playing with Chicago?
A   He started in 1902 and played through 1912. He went to the Reds and then to the Federal League. He came back to the Cubs and played his last season in 1916.

Q   Within 10 points, what was Joe Tinker's lifetime batting average?
A   .263

Q   What were two nicknames for the Chicago Cubs team before "Cubs" was made official?
A   "Colts" and "Orphans"

Q   Hank Sauer had a brother who played in the National League. What was his name?
A   Ed. He played with the Cubs in 1943, 1944, and 1945, and later with the Cards and the Boston Braves.

Q   Did Bill Veeck ever own the Chicago Cubs?
A   No

Q   Did Bill Veeck ever work for the Chicago Cubs?
A   Yes. He started out as the stock boy and worked his way to club treasurer. His father was president of the club.

Q   Did Chuck Klein ever play for the Cubs?
A   Yes. He played for the Cubs in 1934, 1935, and part of 1936.

Q   How did the Cubs obtain Chuck Klein?
A   He was traded in November, 1933 by the Philadelphia Phillies along with Mark Koenig, Harvey Hendrick, Ted Kleinhans, and a bundle of cash.

Q Was Chuck Klein in any World Series with the Cubs?
A Yes. He played in the outfield in 1935 when the Cubs played the Tigers.

Q Did Chuck Klein ever lead the National League in batting?
A Yes, in 1933.

Q Did Chuck Klein ever lead the league in runs batting it?
A Yes, in 1931 and 1933.

Q Who was "Highpockets" Kelly?
A George "Highpockets" Kelly was a first baseman who played in the National League for 16 years. He was with the Chicago Cubs briefly in 1930. He entered baseball's Hall of Fame in 1973.

Q Who was Mike Kelly?
A Mike Kelly was better known as "King." He was with Chicago in the old National League, from 1880 to 1886.

Q Who prompted the famous baseball expression, "Slide, Kelly, slide."
A Mike Kelly.

Q Is Mike Kelly in the Hall of Fame?
A Yes, he was inducted in 1945.

Q How many years did "Gabby" Hartnett catch for the Cubs?
A 19 years

Q Where did Hartnett go after he left the Cubs?
A New York Giants

Q Is Hartnett in baseball's Hall of Fame?
A Yes. He went in in 1955.

Q What years did "Gabby" manage the Cubs?
A 1938, 1939, and 1940

Q   Within 10 points, what was Hartnett's lifetime batting average?
A   .297

Q   Did "Gabby" ever play in a World Series for the Cubs?
A   Yes. He was in four World Series.

Q   What were the years that Hartnett was in a World Series?
A   1929, 1932, 1935, and 1938

Q   Did Hartnett ever hit a homerun in the World Series?
A   Yes, two. He hit one in the 1932 World Series and again in the 1935 World Series.

Q   Did Hartnett ever play any other position but catcher?
A   Yes. In his second year, 1923, he played first base in 31 games. In 1932 he played one game at first base and in 1940, one game at third base.

Q   Did Monty Irvin ever play with the Chicago Cubs?
A   Yes, in 1956.

Q   Who was the future Chicago Cub who stole home in the 19(?- World Series against the Yankees when he was playing for the Philadelphia Phillies?
A   Monty Irvin

Q   Is Monty Irvin in the Hall of Fame?
A   Yes; he was inducted in 1973.

Q   When did the Cubs start playing at Wrigley Field?
A   The first National League game played at Wrigley Field took place in 1916. It was then known as Weeghman Park and would later be called Cubs Park. In 1926 it was officially named Wrigley Field.

Q   In what year was Wrigley Field double-decked?
A   Before the opening game in 1928.

18

Q   What three men have pinch-hit grand slam homeruns in their careers? One of them was a former Cub. Who are they?

A   Ron Northey, Willie McCovey, and Rich Reese.

Q   How old was Fred Lindstrom when he first appeared in a World Series?

A   He was 18 years old and would be 19 a month later when he played for the Giants in 1924.

Q   Where did Fred Lindstrom coach baseball after his retirement?

A   At Northwestern University in Evanston.

Q   Is Fred Lindstrom in baseball's Hall of Fame?

A   Yes; he was admitted in 1976.

Q   How many games did "Three Finger" Brown win in his major league career?

A   239

Q   Was "Three Finger" Brown ever in a World Series with the Cubs?

A   He was with the Cubs in 1906, 1907, 1908, and 1910, when they won the pennants, and he won five games and lost four in the World Series.

Q   Why was "Three Finger" Brown called "Three Finger"?

A   Because as a youth he lost parts of two fingers in a feed cutter accident.

Q   Is "Three Finger" Brown a member of baseball's Hall of Fame?

A   He was admitted to baseball's Hall of Fame in 1949.

Q   Clark Griffith is best known as the owner of the Washington Senators. Did he ever play baseball?

A   He won 20 more games for the Chicago National Leagues for six years in a row. He was the pitcher and manager of the Chicago American League entry in 1901.

Q   Did Burleigh Grimes ever pitch for the Cubs?

A   Yes. Grimes pitched briefly for the Cubs in 1932 and 1933.

Q   What Cub hit homeruns four times in a row?

A   On July 22 and July 23, 1944, Billy Nicholson hit four consecutive homeruns.

Q   What was Bob Buhl's claim to fame as a "hitter"?

A   Bob pitched for both the Milwaukee Braves and Chicago Cubs, and in 1962 he went to bat 70 times and never got a hit, creating a big league record for most at-bats in a season without a hit.

Q   Who was the Philadelphia Philly first baseman who was shot in a Chicago hotel by a young woman?

A   Eddie Waitkus, who started his career with the Cubs in 1941. In June of 1949, he received a note from a stranger who wrote that she wanted to see him as soon as possible, saying that it was "extremely important." When Waitkus knocked at the door, he was admitted and immediately shot. Waitkus recovered and came back in 1950 to hit .284.

Q   What are the words to the poem about Tinker, Evers, and Chance?

A   "These are the saddest of possible words/Tinkers to Evers to Chance./Trio of bear cubs and fleeter than birds/Tinkers to Evers to Chance./Thoughtlessly pricking our gonfalon bubble/making a Giant hit into a double./Words that are weighty with nothing but trouble/Tinkers to Evers to Chance."

Q   The old National League was founded in 1876. Up until 1900 how many times did a Chicago National League player lead the league?

A   Six times. Cap Anson led it three times, King Kelly once, George Gore and Roscoe Barnes, each once.

Q   How many times has a Cub led the National League in batting since 1900?

A   Heinie Zimmerman was the first in 1912; Phil Cavarretta in 1945; Billy Williams in 1972; Bill Madlock in 1975 and 1976; and Bill Buckner in 1980.

Q   Since 1900, how many Cubs have won the Homerun Championship?

A   Frank "Wildfire" Shulte won in 1911 and tied for the leadership in 1910. Heinie Zimmerman won in 1912. Cy Williams was tied for the title in 1916. Hack Wilson won the championship in 1926, 1928, and 1930, and tied in 1927. Billy Nicholson won it in 1943 and 1944. Hank Sauer tied in 1952. Ernie Banks won the championship in 1958 and 1960. Dave Kingman won in 1979 and Andre Dawson in 1987.

Q   How many Cub pitchers have pitched no-hitters since 1900?

A   Cub pitchers have pitched ten no-hitters, including two by Ken Holtzman. Others are Bob Wicker, Leonard Cole, Jim Lavender, Jim Vaughn, Sam Jones, Don Cardwell, Burt Hooton, and Milt Pappas.

Q   Has a Cub first baseman ever played a game without having a fielding chance?

A   Yes. On June 29, 1937, "Rip" Collins, playing first base, set a National League record by not having a fielding chance in the game's 11–9 victory over the Cardinals.

Q   Why is Cy Williams remembered as a Cub?

A   He played with the Cubs for six years and one year led the National League with 12 homeruns.

21

Q   What is Eddie Waitkus best remembered for?
A   Waitkus played for the Cubs for four years, but in 1949 he was shot by a deranged woman in the old Edgewater Beach Hotel.

Q   Who was the woman that shot Eddie Watikus?
A   Ruth Steinhagen.

Q   Roger Bresnahan played parts of four years for the Chicago Cubs, but why is he best remembered?
A   He is best remembered as the battery mate of the great Christy Mattheson when they both played for the New York Giants.

Q   Who was John Evers?
A   Evers was the middle man in the famous double-play combination, Tinkers to Evers to Chance.

Q   When did Johnny Evers play for the Chicago Cubs?
A   He came up with Chicago in 1902 and stayed with them through 1913.

Q   Is Johnny Evers in baseball's Hall of Fame?
A   Yes. He was elected in 1946.

Q   Is Frank Chance called the "Peerless Leader" in the baseball's Hall of Fame?
A   Yes. He was admitted to the Hall of Fame in 1946.

Q   When did Kiki Cuyler play for the Cubs?
A   Cuyler came to the Cubs from Pittsburgh in a trade for Sparky Adams and Pete Scott in November 1927.

Q   How long did Kiki Cuyler play for the Cubs?
A   He played with the Cubs from 1928 to the middle of the 1935 season when he went to Cincinnati.

Q   Did Kiki Cuyler ever play in the World Series with the Cubs?
A   Yes. He played with the Cubs in 1929 and 1932 in the World Series. He also played with Pittsburgh in 1925.

Q   Is Kiki Cuyler in the Hall of Fame?
A   Yes. He was admitted to baseball's Hall of Fame in 1968.

Q   Did Joe Tinker ever manage?
A   Yes. He managed the Reds in 1913, Chicago in the Federal League in 1914 and 1915, and the Cubs in 1916.

Q   Is Joe Tinker in the Hall of Fame?
A   Yes; he was admitted in 1948.

Q   Did Rube Waddell ever pitch for Chicago?
A   Yes. He pitched for Chicago in the National League during part of 1901; he won 13 games and lost 15.

Q   Is Rube Waddell in baseball's Hall of Fame?
A   Yes; he was inducted in 1946.

Q   How long did Frank Secory play for the Cubs?
A   Frank was with the Cubs in 1944, 1945, and 1946.

Q   Did Frank Secory ever play in the World Series?
A   Yes. He played in the World Series with the Cubs against the Tigers in 1945 and got two hits in five times at bat.

Q   How long did Frank Secory umpire in the National League?
A   18 years

Q   What former Cub outfielder played third base in the movie "Pride of the Yankees," which starred Gary Cooper as Lou Gehrig?
A   Peanuts Lowrey

Q   What former Cub pitcher had a father who pitched against the Cubs in the 1945 World Series?

A   Steve Trout's father was Paul "Dizzy" Trout, who pitched for the Tigers for many years.

Q   What former Cub player was nicknamed the "Penguin?"

A   Ron Cey

Q   What Cubs pitcher won 20 games in a single season split between two leagues?

A   Hank Borowy pitched for the Yankees in the start of the season in 1945. He had won 10 and lost 5 when he was sold to the Chicago Cubs. He won 11 out of 13 decisions for the Cubs, thus becoming the only pitcher to win 20 games between two leagues, which was the only 20-game season that he ever had. (That was during the last season that the Cubs won the pennant.)

Q   Tony Lazzeri was a Chicago Cub in 1938; with which team did he gain his greatest fame?

A   The New York Yankees

Q   What year did he play for the Cubs?

A   1938

Q   Tony set a record of 11 runs batted in in one game; when did he do it?

A   With the New York Yankees in 1936 on May 24.

Q   Was Mark Koenig with the Cubs in the 1932 World Series?

A   Yes. They played against the Yankees, Mark's former team. Babe Ruth and the other Yankees taunted the Chicago Cubs about being cheap and asked Mark why he didn't come back and play with the Yankees instead of a "cheap" ball club.

24

Q Who was Bobby Sturgeon?
A Bobby Sturgeon came up to the Chicago Cubs in 1940 and played there until 1947, except for three war years, 1943, 1944 and 1945. He was a shortstop.

Q What was Riggs Stephenson's nickname?
A "Old Hoss"

Q How long did Riggs Stephenson play with the Chicago Cubs?
A He came to the Chicago Cubs in 1926 from the Cleveland Indians and played through 1934.

Q Who was the catcher during the era of Tinkers to Evers to Chance?
A Johnny Kling caught from 1902 to 1910.

Q Who were the outfielders who played most of the time during the era of Tinkers to Evers to Chance?
A "Wildfire" Shulte, Jimmy Sheckard, and Jimmy Slagle were the outfielders during this era.

Q In 1935 the Chicago Cubs set their record for most consecutive wins in the season. How many did they win in a row?
A 21

Q In May of 1942 a Boston Brave pitcher hit three homeruns to help defeat the Chicago Cubs at Wrigley Field. Who was that pitcher?
A Jim Tobin

Q On June 25, 1937, a Chicago Cub became the first pinch-hitter to hit one homerun left-handed and one right-handed in the same game. Who was the player?
A Augie Galan

Q Who had the most runs batted in his career with the Cubs?
A Cap Anson, with 1,714; Ernie Banks was second with 1,636.

Q   Who had the highest batting average for his career with the Cubs?

A   Riggs Stephenson, with a .336 batting average.

Q   How old was Phil Cavarratta when he came up with the Cubs?

A   Cavaratta came up as an 18-year-old first baseman with the Chicago Cubs in 1934 and played through 1955.

Q   Who relieved Grimm as manager of the Cubs in 1949?

A   Frank Frisch

Q   Who relieved Frisch as manager of the Cubs in 1951?

A   Phil Cavarratta

Q   Who relieved Phil Cavarratta just before the 1954 season as manager of the Cubs?

A   Stan Hack

Q   How long did Stan Hack manage the Cubs?

A   Three years — 1954, 1955, and 1956.

Q   When did Bob Sheffing pilot the Cubs?

A   In 1957, 1958, and 1959.

Q   Where did the Cubs play before they played at Wrigley Field?

A   Westside Grounds, from 1893 through 1915.

****

As Cubs manager in 1884, Cap Anson was paid the handsome salary of $375.00 a month. His contract charged him 50 cents a day for room and board when the Cubs were on the road.

Bill Veeck planted the ivy on the outfield wall in 1937 when he was a 23-year-old youngster. He strung bittersweet from the top to the bottom of the walls and planted the ivy at the base.

The Cubs got their nickname in 1907. They were once known as the White Stockings, the Colts, and the Orphans.

26

Andre Dawson has a street named after him in the city of South Miami: Andre Dawson Drive. Yes, it is more than 400 feet long.

Ryne Sandberg began his career with the Cubs by going into a 1-for-32 slump.

Hack Wilson hit 57 homers for the Cubs in 1930 but got credit for only 56. He hit one so hard in Cincinnati that it bounced in and out of the seats and the umpires never saw it.

CHAPTER TWO
THE CHICAGO CUBS
IN THE 1950'S

Q   Give the infield of the Chicago Cubs in 1953.
A   At first base was Dee Fondy, second base was Eddie Miksis, shortstop was Roy Smalley, and third base was Ron Jackson.

Q   Who were the main outfielders for the Cubs in 1953?
A   Frank Baumholtz, Ralph Kiner, and Hank Sauer.

Q   Who caught the most games for the Cubs in 1953?
A   Clyde McCullough and Joe Garragiola

Q   Who were the reserves for the Cubs in 1953?
A   Billy Serena in the infield, Joe Garragiola was catcher, and Hal Jeffcoat in the outfield.

Q   Who were the leading pitchers on the Cubs in 1953?
A   Warren Hacker, Paul Minner, Johnny Klippstein, Rob Rush, and Turk Lown.

Q   Who were the main relief pitchers for the Cubs in 1953?
A   Howie Pollet, Dutch Leonard, and Bubba Church.

Q   What position did the Cubs finish in in the National League race in 1954?
A   Seventh

Q   Who was the manager in 1954?
A   Stan Hack

Q   What was the infield of the Cubs in 1954?
A   Dee Fondy was at first, Gene Baker was the second baseman, Ernie Banks was at short, and Ron Jackson at third.

Q   What was the outfield of the Cubs in 1954?
A   Hank Sauer, Ralph Kiner, Dale Talbot.

Q   Who caught most of the games for the Cubs in 1951?
A   Smoky Burgess

Q   Who were some of the reserves for the Cubs in 1951?
A   Phil Cavarrata, Wayne Terwilliger, Dee Fondy, Gene Hermanski.

Q   Who was the leading pitcher on the Cubs in 1951?
A   Bob Rush won 11 and lost 12; Dutch Leonard won 10, lost 6.

Q   Who were some of the pitchers who pitched for the Cubs in 1951?
A   Bob Rush, Paul Minner, Calvin McLish, Frank Hiller, Turk Lown, Johnny Klippstein, Dutch Leonard, and Bob Kelly.

Q   What position did the Cubs finish in in the National League pennant race in 1952?
A   Fifth place

Q   What was the infield of the Chicago Cubs in 1952?
A   Dee Fondy was at first, Eddie Miksis at second, Ron Jackson at third, and Roy Smalley was the shortstop.

Q What was the outfield for the Cubs in 1952?
A Hal Jeffcoat, Hank Sauer, and Frank Baumholtz.

Q Who were the reserves on the Cubs in 1952?
A Billy Serena, Gene Hermanski, Bob Ramazzotti, Bob Addis and Tommy Brown.

Q Who were the main pitchers for the Cubs in 1952?
A Bob Rush, who won 17 and lost 13, Johnny Klipperstein, Warren Hacker, Paul Minner, Turk Lown, Bob Kelly and Dutch Leonard.

Q A Cub pitcher led the National League in strikeouts in 1955. Who was he?
A Sam Jones with 198.

Q How many runs did Ernie Banks drive in during 1955?
A Banks was fourth in the league with 117.

Q How many homeruns did Ernie Banks hit in 1955?
A Ernie was third in the league with 44.

Q Who led the National League in total bases in 1955?
A Willie Mays with 382, and Ernie Banks was third with 355.

Q Where did the Chicago Cubs finish in the National League in 1956?
A Dead last

Q Who comprised the infield in 1956?
A Dee Fondy, G. Baker, Ernie Banks, and Don Hoak were the regulars. Eddie Miksis was a reserve.

Q Who comprised the outfield for the Cubs in 1956?
A Monty Irvin, Pete Whisenant, and Moose Moryn.

Q Who were the utility outfielders in 1956 for the Cubs?
A Jim King and Sam Drake

Q   Who was the regular catcher for the Cubs in 1956?
A   Hobie Landrith

Q   Who was the leading pitcher on the Cubs in 1956?
A   Bob Rush won 13 and lost 10.

Q   How many pitchers on the Cubs won 10 or more games in 1956?
A   Only one, Bob Rush.

Q   What place did the Cubs finish in the National League pennant race in 1958?
A   Fifth

Q   Give the infield of the Cubs in 1958.
A   Dale Long at first, Tony Taylor at second, Alvin Dark at third, Ernie Banks at shortstop.

Q   Who played in the outfield for the Cubs in 1958?
A   Lee Walls, Bobby Thompson, Walt Moryn.

Q   What Cub pitcher won the most games in 1958?
A   Glen Hobbie won 10 games and lost 6. Moe Drabowsky won 9 and lost 11, and Don Elston also won 9 and lost 8.

Q   Who led the National League in homeruns in 1958?
A   Ernie Banks with 47.

Q   Who led the National League in runs batted in during 1958?
A   Ernie Banks, with 129.

Q   Who had the highest slugging average in the National League in 1958?
A   Ernie Banks, with .614.

Q   Who had the most total bases in the National League in 1958?
A   Ernie Banks, with 379.

Q   Who led the National League in stolen bases in 1958?
A   Willie Mays, with 31.

Q   Who led the Chicago Cubs in stolen bases in 1958?
A   Tony Taylor, with 21.

Q   Who scored the most runs in the National League in 1958?
A   Willie Mays had 121 and Ernie Banks had 119.

Q   Bobby Thompson hit the homerun that was heard around the world in 1951 against Brooklyn. Did Thompson ever play for the Cubs?
A   Yes. In 1958 and 1959 Thompson played in the outfield for the Chicago Cubs.

Q   Dale Long, who later played for the Cubs, hit eight homeruns in eight straight games in May of 1956. Who was he playing for at the time?
A   Pittsburgh

Q   Where was Moe Drabowksy born?
A   Moe was born in Poland and came to the United States when he was three years old.

Q   The Cubs had two players on the Sporting News All Star rookie team in 1958. Who were they?
A   Sam Taylor was the catcher and Tony Taylor was the second baseman.

Q   Who was named Chicago Rookie of the Year by the Chicago Baseball Writers Association in 1958?
A   Glen Hobbie

Q   What position did the Cubs finish in the National League in 1950?
A   They were in seventh place.

Q   What was the infield for the Cubs in 1950?

A   The infield was composed of Preston Ward at first base, Wayne Terwilliger at second base, Bill Serena at third base and Roy Smalley as shortstop.

Q   What Cub pitcher led the National League in number of games pitched in 1958?

A   Don Elston with 69.

Q   Where did the Cubs finish in the National League pennant race in 1959?

A   Fifth

Q   Who managed the Cubs in 1959?

A   Bob Scheffing

Q   Who played first base for the Cubs in 1959?

A   Dale Long

Q   Who played second base for the Cubs in 1959?

A   Tony Taylor

Q   Who was the third baseman for the Cubs in 1959?

A   Alvin Dark

Q   Who was the shortstop for the cubs in 1959?

A   Ernie Banks

Q   Who played in the outfield for the Cubs in 1959?

A   Lee Walls, Bobby Thompson, and George Altman.

Q   Who were the utility outfielders for the Cubs in 1959?

A   Walt Moryn and Irv Noren

Q   How many Cub pitchers won over 10 games in 1959?

A   Glen Hobbie won 16, Bob Anderson won 12, and Don Elston won 10.

Q How many times did Ralph Kiner lead the National League in home runs?

A During seven consecutive years (1946–1953) he either led or was tied for the lead.

Q Is "Rabbit" Maranville in baseball's Hall of Fame?

A Yes. He was elected in 1954. Maranville played one season with the Cubs in 1925.

Q How did the Cubs get Ernie Banks?

A On September 8, 1953, they bought a pitcher named Bill Dickey and a skinny shortstop from the Kansas City Monarchs of the Negro American League for $10,000. The shortstop was Ernie Banks.

Q What was Johnny "No-Hit" VanderMeer's other nickname?

A The "Dutch Master"

Q When did Bob Rush pitch for the Cubs?

A From 1948 through 1957

Q Where did Bob Rush go when he left the Cubs?

A He was traded with Eddie Haas and Don Kaiser to Milwaukee for Taylor Phillips and Sammy Taylor in December 1957.

Q What is the most wins that Bob Rush ever had for the Cubs?

A In 1952 he won 17 and lost 13.

Q What was Johnny Schmitz' nickname?

A "Beartracks"

Q What was the last year that Johnny Schmitz pitched for the Cubs?

A 1951. He came up in 1941.

Q What was the most wins that Johnny Schmitz ever had as a Cub?

A He won 18 and lost 13 in 1948.

Q   Who is the only ball player in major league history to appear in a World Series game without having appeared in a regular season game?

A   Clyde McCullough pinch hitted in the 1945 World Series; he had not been in a regular season game because he had been in military service.

Q   Who holds the record in the National League for most grand slams in a season?

A   Ernie Banks, who had five in 1955.

Q   Did Phil Cavarratta ever play for the Chicago White Sox?

A   Yes. He spent his last two years (1954 and 1955) with the White Sox.

Q   Who is the only player in the major leagues to have played all years between 1935, which was Babe Ruth's last, and 1954, which was Hank Aaron's first?

A   Phil Cavarratta

Q   Did Don Zimmer ever play in a World Series?

A   Yes, twice, in 1955 and 1959 while playing for the Dodgers.

Q   Who is the only left-handed catcher in Chicago Cub history?

A   Dale Long caught for the Cubs on August 20, 1958, in the first game of a double-header with Pittsburgh.

Q   What Chicago Cubs of the 1950's were named Most Valuable Players in the National League?

A   Phil Cavarratta and Hank Sauer in 1952, Ernie Banks in 1958 and 1959, Gabby Hartnett in 1935, Ryne Sanberg in 1986, and Andre Dawson in 1987.

Q   Earl Averill was a Hall of Fame outfielder playing with the Cleveland Indians, Detroit Tigers, and the Boston Braves. Did he ever have a son who played for the Cubs?

A   Yes. Earl Averill, son of Earl Howard Averill, played for the Cubs in 1959 and 1960. He was mainly a catcher.

Q   Who was the second highest winner of games for the Cubs in 1956?

A   "Sad Sam" Jones won nine, and so did Turk Lown.

Q   Who were some of the pitchers who pitched for the Cubs in 1956?

A   Jim Brosnan, Vito Valentinette, Turk Lown, Bob Rush, "San Sam" Jones, Don Kaiser, Jim Davis, and Warren Hacker.

Q   What Cub pitcher led the National League in strikeouts in 1956?

A   "Sad Sam" Jones, with 176.

Q   What Cub pitcher was third in the National League in saves in 1956?

A   Turk Lown, with 13.

Q   What position did the Cubs finish in the National League pennant race in 1957?

A   Seventh

Q   Who was the manager of the Cubs in 1957?

A   Bob Scheffing

Q   Did Chuck Tanner ever play for the Cubs?

A   Yes. He played with the Cubs in 1958.

Q   Did Chuck Tanner ever manage the Cubs?

A   No. He managed the White Sox from 1970 through 1975.

Q   Name the infield of the Cubs in 1956.

A   Dale Long at first, Bobby Morgan at second, Bobby Adams at third, and Ernie Banks at short.

Q   In 1952 Bob Rush won 17 games for the Cubs. How many complete games did he have?

A   17

Q   In 1952 Warren Hacker won 15 games and lost 9 for the Cubs. He had a 2.58 earned run average. Was this the lowest in the National League?

A   No. Hoyt Wilhelm had the lowest in the league with a 2.43. Hacker was second.

Q   Who was the first Chicago Cub to be named Player of the Year?

A   Henry Sauer, in 1952.

Q   Was Ernie Banks ever named Player of the Year?

A   Yes, twice: 1958 and 1959.

Q   Who was Vance Law's father?

A   Vance is the son of Vernon Law, who pitched for the Pirates from 1950 to 1951 and from 1954 to 1967. He was a Cy Young winner.

Q   Stan Musial made only one pitching appearance in his big league career. When was that?

A   That was in September of 1952 against the Chicago Cubs.

Q   Who was the only batter in the Major Leagues to face Stan Musial in his one pitching performance?

A   Frank Baumholtz reached first base on an error. He was the only man Musial ever pitched to.

Q   What Cub manager was replaced just before the 1954 season started?

A   Phil Cavarratta was replaced by Stan Hack.

Q   Bob Rush was tied for third with the most number of wins in the National League in 1952. How many did he have?

A   Rush had 17 wins.

Q   Bob Rush was fifth in the National League in number of complete games in 1952. How many did he have?

A   Seventeen

Q Dutch Leonard was tied for third for number of saves in the National League in 1952. How many did he have?
A 11

Q Who led the National League in homeruns in 1952?
A Hank Sauer, with 37, tied with Ralph Kiner.

Q Who led the National League in runs batted in during 1952?
A Hank Sauer, with 121.

Q Who had the highest slugging average in the National League in 1952?
A Stan Musial of the Cards had .538, and Hank Sauer was second with .531.

Q Who led the National League in batting in 1952?
A Stan Musial with .336, and Frank Baumholtz of the Cubs was second with .325.

Q What position did the Chicago Cubs finish in during the National League pennant race in 1953?
A Seventh

Q Name the outfield of the Cubs in 1957.
A Walt Moryn, Chuck Tanner, and Lee Walls.

Q Name some of the reserves of the Cubs in 1957.
A Bob Speake, Jerry Kindall, and Jim Bolger.

Q Who was the main catcher for the Cubs in 1957?
A Cal Neeman

Q Who were the leading pitchers for the Cubs in 1957?
A Dick Drott won 15 and lost 11, and Moe Drabowsky won 13 and lost 15.

Q   Who were the seven most active pitchers with the Cubs in 1957?

A   Dick Drott, Bob Rush, Moe Drabowsky, Jim Brosnan, Turk Lown, Don Elston, and Dave Hillman.

Q   How many homeruns did Ernie Banks have in 1957?

A   Ernie had 43 and finished one behind Hank Aaron who had 44.

Q   How many runs batted in did Ernie Banks have in 1957?

A   102. Hank Aaron led the league with 132.

Q   What pitcher led the National League in strikeouts in 1957?

A   Jack Sanford of the Philadelphia Phillies, and Dick Drott and Moe Drabowsky were tied for second. They each had 170 and Sanford had 188.

Q   What Cub pitcher pitched in the most games in the National League in 1957?

A   Turk Lown appeared in 67 games.

Q   Who managed the Cubs in 1958?

A   Bob Scheffing

Q   Give the lineup for the 1959 Chicago Cubs opening day.

A   Tony Taylor, second base; Altman, centerfield; Banks, shortstop; Moryn, leftfield; Averill, third base; Long, first base; Thompson, rightfield; Sam Taylor, catcher; Anderson, pitcher.

Q   When did Sam Jones pitch a no-hit game for the Cubs?

A   May 12, 1955.

Q   When Sam Jones pitched his no-hit game, where was the game played?

A   Wrigley Field in Chicago

Q   Stan Musial got his 3000th hit off a Cub pitcher. Who was the pitcher?

A   Moe Drabowsky. The date was May 13, 1958.

Q   When Stan Musial got his 3000th hit, where was the game played?

A   In Chicago, at Wrigley Field.

Q   On May 21, 1955, Warren Hacker came close to a no-hitter. What happened?

A   George Crowe got the only hit of the game with one out in the ninth, and the Cubs beat the Braves 2–1 in Milwaukee.

Q   What Cub got a homerun in his first time at bat and a triple in the second time at bat?

A   Frank Ernaga got a homerun and then a triple as the Cubs beat Milwaukee 5–1 on May 24, 1957.

Q   Who were the main catchers for the Cubs in 1954?

A   Joe Garagiola, Elvin Tappe, and Clyde McCullough.

Q   Who were the starting pitchers for the Cubs in 1954?

A   Bob Rush, Paul Minner, Warren Hacker, Johnny Klippstein, and Howie Pollet.

Q   Who were the relief pitchers?

A   Dave Cole, Hal Jeffcoat, and Jim Davis.

Q   What position were the Cubs in at the end of the 1955 pennant race?

A   Sixth

Q   Who was the manager of the Cubs in 1955?

A   Stan Hack.

Q   Who were the main pitchers for the Cubs in 1955?

A   "Sad Sam" Jones, Bob Rush, Warren Hacker, Paul Minner, and Jim Davis.

Q   Who were the relief pitchers?
A   Mainly Hal Jeffcoat and Howie Pollet

Q   What was the infield of the Cubs in 1955?
A   Dee Fondy, G. Baker, Ernie Banks, Ron Jackson.

Q   What was the outfield for the Cubs in 1955?
A   Jim King, Hank Sauer, and Eddie Miksis.

Q   Who caught the most games for the Cubs in 1955?
A   Harry Chiti

Q   Who were the reserves for the Cubs in 1955?
A   Framk Baumholtz, Jim Bolger, and Bob Speake.

Q   How many homeruns did Ernie Banks hit in 1959?
A   45

Q   Who led the league in 1959 in homeruns?
A   Eddie Matthews with 46; Ernie Banks was second with 45.

Q   Who led the National League in runs batted in in 1959?
A   Ernie Banks, with 143.

Q   Who led the National League in stolen bases in 1959?
A   Willie Mays had 27; Tony Taylor and Orlando Cepepa and Junior Gilliam were tied for second with 23.

Q   Who led the National League in total bases in 1959?
A   Hank Aaron had 400, Eddie Matthews had 352, and Ernie Banks had 351.

Q   How many times was Ernie Banks selected for the All Star Game?
A   14 times

Q   What Cubs were selected for the All Star Game in 1950?
A   Andy Pakfo, Bob Rush, and Hank Sauer.

Q   What Cubs were selected for the All Star Team in 1951?
A   Bruce Edwards and Dutch Leonard

Q   What Cubs were chosen for the All Star team in 1952?
A   Toby Atwell, Bob Rush, and Hank Sauer.

Q   What member of the Cubs was chosen for the All Star team in 1953?
A   Ralph Kiner

Q   What Cub was chosen for the All Star team in 1954?
A   Randy Jackson

Q   Did Dick Drott ever strike out Hank Aaron four times in one game?
A   Yes. On May 26, 1957, Drott beat the Braves 7–5 at Wrigley Field, striking out 15 batters and Hank Aaron four times.

Q   Did Moose Moryn ever hit three homeruns in one game?
A   Yes, on May 30, 1958, as the Cubs beat the Dodgers in a double-header. Moryn got his homeruns in the second game.

Q   Where did Ernie Banks hit his 100th career homerun?
A   In Philadelphia on June 9, 1957.

Q   Did Hank Sauer ever hit three homeruns off Curt Simmons in one game?
A   Yes, as the Cubs defeated the Phillies 3–0 at Wrigley Field on June 11, 1952, and Hank Sauer hit three homeruns that day.

Q   Where did Ernie Banks hit his 200th homerun?
A   On June 14, 1959, Banks hit number 200 off Carlton Willie at Wrigley Field.

Q   Did Roy Smalley ever hit for the cycle?
A   Yes, on June 28, 1950.

Q   What notable even happened on June 29, 1952, involving the Chicago Cubs?
A   The Cubs had two outs in the ninth, nobody on base, were seven runs behind, and they rallied for seven runs to defeat the Reds in Cincinnati.

Q   Who relieved Grimm as manager of the Cubs in 1949?
A   Frank Frisch

Q   Who relieved Frisch as manager of the Cubs in 1951?
A   Phil Cavarratta

Q   Who relieved Phil Cavarratta just before the 1954 season as manager of the Cubs?
A   Stan Hack

Q   How long did Stan Hack manage the Cubs?
A   Three years: 1954, 1955, and 1956.

Q   When did Bob Scheffing pilot the Cubs?
A   1957, 1958, 1959, and part of 1960.

Q   When was Bill Serena with the Cubs?
A   Serena played with the Cubs from 1949 through 1954.

Q   What was Serena's lifetime batting average in the major leagues?
A   .251

Q   How long did Roy Smalley play for the Chicago Cubs?
A   He played with the Cubs from 1948 through 1953.

Q   Roy Smalley was traded in March of 1954 to Milwaukee. What did the Cubs receive in exchange?
A   Dave Cole and cash

44

Q   Did Bob Rush ever get credit for winning in an All Star game?
A   Yes, July 8, 1952. Rush was the winning pitcher in the game played that day.

Q   When did Billy Williams join the Chicago Cubs?
A   August 6, 1959.

Q   What player has appeared in the most games in a Cub uniform?
A   Ernie Banks, who played in 2,528 games.

Q   In June of 1953 the Cubs made a big trade with Pittsburgh. Whom did they trade and whom did they get?
A   Howie Pollet, Joe Garagiola, "Catfish" Metkovich, and Ralph Kiner came to Chicago in exchange for Bob Schultz, Preston Ward, George Freese, Bob Addis, Gene Hermanski, and Toby Atwell and cash.

Q   Did Johnny VanderMeer ever pitch for the Cubs?
A   He came to the Cubs in 1950, then went to Cleveland, and finished his career in 1951.

Q   Why is Johnny VanderMeer immortal in baseball history?
A   He pitched two consecutive no-hit games for Cincinnati in 1938.

Q   Did Monty Irvin ever play for the Cubs?
A   Yes, in 1956.

Q   Is Monty Irvin in the Hall of Fame?
A   Yes, in 1973.

Q   What future Cub stole home in the 1951 World Series when he was a member of the New York Giants?
A   Monty Irvin

Q What years did Ralph Kiner play for the Cubs?
A He came to Chicago in 1953 and played there through 1954.

Q Is Ralph Kiner in baseball's Hall of Fame?
A He was elected in 1975.

Q Who were the regular players in the Cubs infield in 1955?
A Dee Fondy, first base; Gene Baker, second base; Ron Jackson at third; and Ernie Banks at shortstop.

Q Who were the main outfielders for the Cubs in 1955?
A Jim King, Eddie Miksis, and Hank Sauer.

Q Who were the reserve outfielders for the Cubs in 1955?
A Frank Baumholtz, Bob Speake, and Jim Bolger.

Q Who was the regular catcher of the Cubs in 1955?
A Harry Chiti

Q Who was the Cub's regular shortstop before Ernie Banks?
A Roy Smalley

Q What was the highest batting average Ernie Banks had during his career?
A In 1958 he hit 313, which was the highest he ever had during his 18 years as a regular with the Cubs.

Q Who were the main outfielders for the Cubs in 1950?
A Andy Pafko, Hank Sauer, and Bob Borkowski.

Q Who is the catcher who caught the most games for the Cubs in 1950?
A Mickey Owen

Q What is Mickey Owen infamous for?
A He missed a called strike in the 1941 World Series that enabled the Yankees to go on to victory.

Q   Who were the reserves of the 1950 Cubs?
A   Phil Cavaratta, Ron Northey, Hank Edwards, Rube Walker, Hal Jeffcoat, and Carmen Mauro.

Q   Who were the starting pitchers for the Cubs in 1950?
A   Bob Rush, Johnny Schmitz, Paul Minner, Frank Hiller, Walt Dubiel.

Q   Who were the relief pitchers for the Cubs in 1950?
A   Doyle Lade, Johnny Klippstein, and Dutch Leonard.

Q   What position did the Cubs finish in the 1951 pennant race in the National League?
A   Last

Q   What was the infield of the 1951 Chicago Cubs?
A   Chuck Conners was at first, Eddie Miksis was at second, Ron Jackson was at third, and Roy Smalley was at short.

Q   Why is the name Chuck Conners familiar to people today?
A   He played "The Rifleman" on TV.

Q   Who were the main outfielders for the Cubs in 1951?
A   Hal Jeffcoat, Frank Baumholtz, and Hank Sauer.

Q   What Cubs were chosen for the All Star game in 1955?
A   Gene Baker, Ernie Banks, Randy Jackson, and "Sad Sam" Jones.

Q   In 1957 what Cub was chosen for the All-Star team?
A   Ernie Banks

Q   In 1958 what Cubs were chosen for the All Star team?
A   Ernie Banks, Walt Moryn, and Lee Walls.

Q   In 1959 there were two All Star games. What Cubs were chosen for the first game?
A   Ernie Banks and Don Elston

Q   In 1959 there were two All Star games. What Cub was chosen for the All Star team?
A   Ernie Banks

Q   Give the opening day lineup for the Cubs in 1957.
A   Fondy, first base; Wise, second base; Will, centerfield; Banks, shortstop; Baker, third base; Bolger, leftfield; Moryn, rightfield; Neeman, catcher; Rush, pitcher.

Q   Give the opening day lineup for the Cubs in 1958.
A   Tony Taylor, second base; Walls, rightfield; Banks, shortstop; Moryn, leftfield; Thompson, centerfield; Long, first base; Goryl, third base; Neeman, catcher; Brosnan, pitcher.

Q   Who won the National League pennant in 1950?
A   The Philadelphia Phillies

Q   Who won the National League pennant in 1951?
A   The New York Giants

Q   Who won the National League pennant in 1952?
A   The Brooklyn Dodgers

Q   Who won the National League pennant in 1953?
A   The Brooklyn Dodgers

Q   Who won the National League pennant in 1954?
A   The New York Giants

Q   Who won the National League pennant in 1955?
A   The Brooklyn Dodgers

Q   Who won the National League pennant in 1956?
A   The Brooklyn Dodgers

Q   Who won the National League pennant in 1957?
A   The Milwaukee Braves

Q Who won the National League pennant in 1958?
A The Milwaukee Braves

Q Who won the National League pennant in 1959?
A The Los Angeles Dodgers

Q Who won the National League batting championship in 1950?
A Stan Musial, with .346.

Q Who won the National League batting championship in 1951?
A Stan Musial (.355)

Q Who won the National League batting championship in 1952?
A Stan Musial (.336)

Q Who won the National League batting championship in 1953?
A Carl Furillo (.344)

Q Who won the National League batting championship in 1954?
A Willie Mays (.345)

Q Who won the National League batting crown in 1955?
A Richie Ashburn (.338)

Q Who won the National League batting championship in 1956?
A Hank Aaron (.328)

Q Who won the batting title in the National League in 1957?
A Stan Musial (.351)

49

Q   Who won the batting crown in the National League in 1958?
A   Richie Ashburn (.350)

Q   Who won the batting title in 1959 in the National League?
A   Hank Aaron (.355)

CHAPTER THREE
THE CHICAGO CUBS
IN THE 1960'S

Q   What Cub pitcher making his first start pitched a no-run, no-hit game in defeating the Cardinals in Wrigley Field 4–0?

A   Don Cardwell, on May 15, 1960. It was the second game of a double header.

Q   In 1965 the Chicago Cubs defense made three triple plays. Who was the Cubs pitcher who was on the mound for each of them?

A   Bill Faul

Q   Did Lew Burdette pitch for the Cubs?

A   Yes. He came to the Cubs from the Cardinals in 1964 and stayed through the 1965 season.

Q   How many games did Lew Burdette win in his 18 years in the Majors?

A   203

Q   How long was Glenn Beckert with the Cubs?

A   He joined the Cubs in 1965 and remained with them through 1973.

Q   On July 4, 1966, who set a modern Cub record by hitting in his 28th straight game?

A   Ron Santo. The Cubs played a double-header that day and Santo was held hitless in the second game.

Q   Rookie Jimmy Qualls had a one-out single in the ninth inning on July 9, 1969, to spoil a no-hit game by the oppositions pitcher. Who was the pitcher?

A   Tom Seaver, as the Mets beat the Cubs 4-0 at Shea Stadium.

Q   Bruce Sutter gained the credit for the All Star Game on July 11, 1978. What did he do?

A   He retired Jim Rice and four other batters.

Q   In the All Star Game on July 11, 1960, who was the hero?

A   Ernie Banks hit a double and a homerun, and then drove in two runs as the National League won 5-3.

Q   Did Billy Williams ever hit for the cycle?

A   Yes, on July 17, 1966.

Q   Where did Ernie Banks collect his 2,000th hit?

A   At Wrigley Field on July 20, 1966.

Q   Ed Bailey had a big day on July 22, 1965. What did he do?

A   Ed had a grand slam homerun and drove in eight runs as the Cubs beat the Phillies at Wrigley Field.

Q   Who was the leading hitter for the Cubs in 1964?

A   Ron Santo (.313)

Q   Who was the leading hitter for the Cubs in 1965?

A   Billy Williams (.315)

Q   Who was the leading hitter for the Cubs in 1966?

A   Ron Santo (.312)

Q   Who was the leading hitter for the Cubs in 1967?
A   Ron Santo (.300)

Q   Who was the leading hitter for the Cubs in 1968?
A   Glen Beckert (.294)

Q   Who was the leading hitter for the Cubs in 1969?
A   Billy Williams (.293)

Q   Who was the leader in number of hits for the Cubs in 1960?
A   Ernie Banks, with 162.

Q   Who was the leader in number of hits for the Cubs in 1961?
A   Ron Santo (.164)

Q   Who was the leader in number of hits for the Cubs in 1962?
A   Billy Williams (.184)

Q   Who was the leader in number of hits for the Cubs in 1963?
A   Ron Santo (.187)

Q   Who was the leader in number of hits for the Cubs in 1964?
A   Billy Williams (.201)

Q   Who was the leader in number of hits for the Cubs in 1965?
A   Billy Williams (.203)

Q   Who was the leader in number of hits for the Cubs in 1966?
A   Glen Beckert (.188)

Q   Who had the most doubles in 1960?
A   Ernie Banks, with 32.

Q   Who had the most doubles in 1961?
A   Ron Santo, with 32.

Q   Who had the most doubles in 1962?
A   George Altman, with 27.

Q   Who had the most doubles in 1963?
A   Billy Williams, with 36.

Q   Who had the most doubles in 1964?
A   Billy Williams, with 39.

Q   Who had the most doubles in 1965?
A   Billy Williams, with 39.

Q   Who had the most doubles in 1966?
A   Adolfo Phillips, with 29.

Q   Who had the most doubles in 1967?
A   Glen Beckert, with 32.

Q   Who had the most doubles in 1968?
A   Billy Williams, with 30.

Q   Who had the most doubles in 1969?
A   Don Kessinger, with 38.

Q   Who was the homerun leader in 1960?
A   Ernie Banks, with 41.

Q   Who was the homerun leader in 1961?
A   Ernie Banks, with 29.

Q   Who was the homerun leader in 1962?
A   Ernie Banks, with 37.

Q   Name the opening day lineup for 1965.
A   Beckert, second base; Pena, shortstop; Williams, centerfield; Santo, third base; Altman, leftfield; Banks, first base; Clemens, rightfield; Bertell, catcher; Ellsworth, pitcher.

Q   Name the opening day lineup for 1966.
A   Cline, centerfield; Beckert, second base; Williams, rightfield; Santo, third base; Altman, leftfield; Banks, first base; Hundley, catcher; Kessinger, shortstop; Jackson, pitcher.

Q   Name the opening day lineup for 1967.
A   Kessinger, shortstop; Beckert, second base; Williams, leftfield; Santo, third base; Banks, first base; Thomas, rightfield; Bertell, catcher; Phillips, centerfield; Jenkins, pitcher.

Q   Name the opening day lineup for 1968.
A   Johnson, rightfield; Kessinger, shortstop; Williams, leftfield; Santo, third base; Banks, first base; Hundley, catcher; Arcia, second base; Phillips, centerfield; Jenkins, pitcher.

Q   Name the opening day lineup for 1969.
A   Kessinger, shortstop; Beckert, second base; Williams, leftfield; Santo, third base; Banks, first base; Hundley, catcher; Hickman, rightfield; Young, centerfield; Jenkins, pitcher.

Q   Who was the manager of the Cubs in 1969?
A   Leo Durocher

Q   Name the opening day lineup for 1960.
A   Ashburn, centerfield; Taylor, second base; Will, rightfield; Banks, shortstop; Thomas, leftfield; Altman, first base; Zimmer, third base; Neeman, catcher; Anderson, pitcher.

Q   Name the opening day lineup for 1961.
A   Ashburn, leftfield; Zimmer, second base; Williams, rightfield;
     Banks, shortstop; Santo, third base; Heist, centerfield; Rodgers, first base; Thacker, catcher; Hobbie, pitcher.

Q   Name the opening day lineup for 1962.
A   Brock, centerfield; Hubbs, second base; Williams, leftfield; Banks, first base; Altman, rightfield; Santo, third base; White, shortstop; Barragan, catcher; Cardwell, pitcher.

Q Name the opening day lineup for 1963.
A Landrum, centerfield; Rodgers, shortstop; Williams, left-field; Santo, third base; Banks, first base; Brock, rightfield; Hubbs, second base; Bertell, catcher; Jackson, pitcher.

Q Name the opening day lineup for 1964.
A Stewart, second base; Brock, rightfield; Williams, leftfield; Santo, third base; Banks, first base; Rodgers, shortstop' Cowan, centerfield; Bertell, catcher; Norman, pitcher.

Q What position did the Cubs finish in 1960?
A Seventh

Q What position did the Cubs finish in 1961?
A Seventh

Q What position did the Cubs finish in 1962?
A Ninth

Q What position did the Cubs finish in 1963?
A Seventh

Q What position did the Cubs finish in 1964?
A Eighth

Q What position did the Cubs finish in 1965?
A Eighth

Q What position did the Cubs finish in 1966?
A Tenth

Q What position did the Cubs finish in 1967?
A Third

Q What position did the Cubs finish in 1968?
A Third

Q   What position did the Cubs finish in 1969?
A   Second in the East Division

Q   Who was the manager of the Cubs in 1966?
A   Leo Durocher

Q   Who was the manager of the Cubs in 1967?
A   Leo Durocher

Q   Who was the manager of the Cubs in 1968?
A   Leo Durocher

Q   Who were the homerun leaders in 1963?
A   Ron Santo and Billy Williams, with 25 each.

Q   Who was the homerun leader in 1964?
A   Billy Williams, with 33.

Q   Who was the homerun leader in 1965?
A   Billy Williams, with 34.

Q   Who was the homerun leader in 1966?
A   Ron Santo, with 30.

Q   Who was the homerun leader in 1967?
A   Ron Santo, with 31.

Q   Who was the homerun leader in 1968?
A   Ernie Banks, with 32.

Q   Who was the homerun leader in 1969?
A   Ron Santo, with 29.

Q   How many Cubs hit grand slams in 1960?
A   Two, Ernie Banks and Ron Santo.

Q   How many Cubs hit grand slams in 1961?
A   Al Heist, Billy Williams twice, and Ernie Banks, again.

Q   How many Cubs hit grand slams in 1962?
A   Lou Brock and Nellie Mathews

Q   How many Cubs hit grand slams in 1963?
A   Ellie Burton and Ron Santo

Q   How many Cubs hit grand slams in 1964?
A   Joe Amalfitano, Billy Williams, and Ernie Banks.

Q   How many Cubs hit grand slams in 1965?
A   Ed Bailey and Billy Williams

Q   How many Cubs hit grand slams in 1966?
A   Randy Hundley

Q   How many Cubs hit grand slams in 1967?
A   Randy Hundley and Adolfo Phillips

Q   How many Cubs hit grand slams in 1968?
A   Ernie Banks, Billy Williams, and Ron Santo.

Q   How many Cubs hit grand slams in 1969?
A   Ernie Banks, Jim Hickman, and Randy Hundley.

Q   Who hit pinch-hit homeruns in 1960?
A   Walt Moryn, Earl Averill, and Sammy Taylor.

Q   Who hit pinch-hit homeruns in 1961?
A   Ernie Banks and Don Zimmer

Q   Who hit pinch-hit homeruns in 1962?
A   Bob Will, twice; Ernie Banks and Dick Bertell.

Q   Who hit pinch-hit homeruns in 1963?
A   Merit Renew and Leo Burke

Q   Who hit pinch-hit homeruns in 1964?
A   Leo Burke and Len Gabrielson

CHICAGO BALL CLUB, 1888.

Jos. Hall, Photo., Brooklyn, N. Y.

6. Capt. Anson
7. Van Haltren.
8. Borchers.
9. Burns.
10. Daly

Ryan.
Williamson.
Farrell.
Pfeffer.
Tec. Maso?

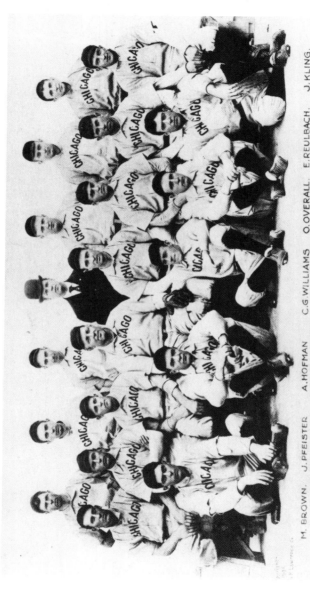

M. BROWN.   J. PFEISTER.   A. HOFFMAN   C.G WILLIAMS   O. OVERALL.   E. REULBACH.   J. KLING.
H. GESSLER.   J. TAYLOR.   H. STEINFELDT.   J. McCORMICK. F. CHANCE.   J. SHECKARD.   P. MORAN.   F. SCHULTE.
C. LUNDGREN.   T. WALSH.   J. EVERS.   J. SLAGLE.   J. TINKER.

CHICAGO NATIONAL LEAGUE BALL CLUB 1906

Credit: NBL

blished by
sehall Magazine Company New York

Enlarged from original
© P. and A. P

Chicago "Cubs", National League Champions, 1929

Front Row (left to right)—Heathcote, English, Cvengros, Beck, Tommy Langtry (Bat Boy), McMillan, Bush, Moore, Stephenson.

Second Row—Jimmie Burke (Coach), Grover Land (Coach), Bob Lewis (Traveling Secretary), Bob Dorr (Groundkeeper), John Seys (Vice-President), William Veeck (President), Miss Donohue (Secretary), William Wrigley, Jr. (Owner), Joe McCarthy (Manager), Hornsby, Cuyler, Wilson.

Back Row—Schulte, Hartnett, Penner, Blake, Blair, Root, Taylor, Latshaw (Trainer), Gramp, Gonzales, Carlson, Tolson, and Malone.

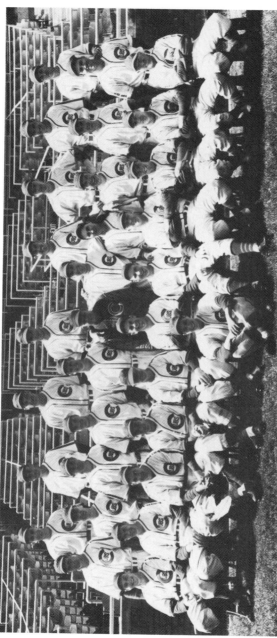

THE CHICAGO CUBS
1938

LOGAN, HACK, BRYANT, EPPERLY, GALAN, MARTY, CARLETON, MATTICK,
RUSSELL, JURGES, REYNOLDS, GARBARK, KIMBALL, LOTSHAW, DEAN, COLLINS, TRIPLETT, O'DEA, ASBELL,
DEMAREE, LEE, FRENCH, LAZZERI, CORRIDEN, GRIMM, JOHNSON, HARTNETT, CAVARRETTA, HERMAN, ROOT,
LAPORTA

Credit: NBL

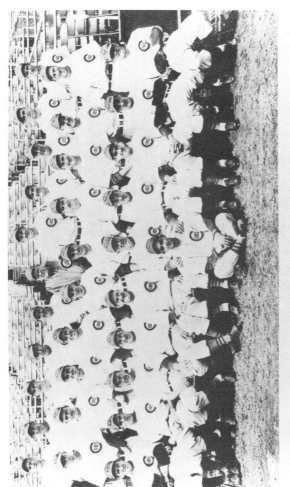

CHICAGO CUBS—1945

FRONT ROW—left to right: Paul Derringer, Mickey Livingston, Stanley Hack, Roy Johnson, Milt Stock, Charlie Grimm, Jimmie Chaliks, Bat Boy—seated on ground, Len Rice, Lennie Merullo, Phil Cavarretta, Claude Passeau.

SECOND ROW—left to right: Loyd Christopher, Paul Gillespie, Don Johnson, Andy Pafko, Harry "P.Nuts" Lowrey, Bill Schuster, Eddie Sauer, Dewey Williams, Ray Prim, Harold H. Vandenberg.

BACK ROW—left to right: Paul Erickson, Frank Secory, Eddie Hanyzewski, Bill Nicholson, Hank Wyse, Andy Lotshaw, Heinz Becker, George Hennessey, Red Smith, Bob Chipman, Mack Stewart.

Credit: NBL

FRONT ROW (L to R) Ernie Banks, Bill Faul, Randy Hundley, Whitey Lockman (Coach), Steve Lillie (Batboy) Leo Durocher (Manager), Fred Fitzsimmons (Coach), Richard Eberle (Batboy), Verlon Walker (Coach), Jimmy Stewart, Billy Williams.

MIDDLE ROW (L to R) Al Scheuneman (Trainer), Joe Proski (Asst. Trainer), Yosh Kawano (Equipment Manager), Marty Keough, Byron Browne, Lee Thomas, Ferguson Jenkins, Dick Ellsworth, Billy Hoeft, George Altman, Ron Santo, Adolfo Phillips, Blake C. .en (Traveling Secretary).

BACK ROW (L to R) Ernie Broglio, Don Lee, Bill Hands, Glenn Beckert, Don Kessinger, Bob Hendley, John Boccabella, Calvin Koonce, Ken Holtzman, Joe Amalfitano, Don Pinkus (Batting Practice Catcher).

Credit: NBL

1989 CHICAGO CUBS

Front row: Bat boys, 2nd row: Mark Grace, Damon Berryhill, Dick Pole (pitching coach) Larry Cox (catchers) Don Zimmer, Mgr., Chuck Cottier, Joe Altobelli, Jose Martinez, Shawon Dunston, Andre Dawson, Ryne Sandburg. 3rd row: _____, _____, Doug Dascenzo, Darrin Jackson, Jeff Pico, Mitch Williams, Calvin Schiraldi, Rick Sutcliffe, Scott Sanderson, Vance Law, Steve Wilson, Domingo Ramos, Jerome Walton, Piersall?, _____. Back row: Rick Wrona, Curtis Wilkerson, Gary Varsho, Lloyd McClendon, Pat Perry, Paul Kilgus, Mike Bielecki, Mitch Webster, Phil Stephenson, Dwight Smith, Greg Maddux.

Not pictured: Joe Girardi, Les Lancaster, Dean Wilkins, Greg Smith, Luis Salazar, Paul Assenmacher.

Credit: NBL

Wrigley Field, Home of the Chicago Cubs, 1945

Credit: NBL

Q   Who hit pinch-hit homeruns in 1965?
A   Len Gabrielson and George Altman

Q   Who hit pinch-hit homeruns in 1966?
A   George Altman and Adolfo Phillips

Q   Who hit pinch-hit homeruns in 1967?
A   Ted Savage and Clarence Jones

Q   Who were the leaders in number of hits for the Cubs in 1967?
A   Ron Santo and Billy Williams, with 176.

Q   Who was the leader in number of hits for the Cubs in 1968?
A   Glen Beckert, with 189.

Q   Who was the leader in number of hits for the Cubs in 1969?
A   Billy Williams, with 188.

Q   Who had the most triples in 1960?
A   Bob Will, with nine.

Q   Who had the most triples in 1961?
A   George Altman, with 12.

Q   Who had the most triples in 1962?
A   Ken Hubbs, with nine.

Q   Who had the most triples in 1963?
A   Lou Brock, with 11.

Q   Who had the most triples in 1964?
A   Ron Santo, with 13.

Q   Who had the most triples in 1965?
A   Billy Williams, with six.

Q   Who had the most triples in 1966?
A   Ron Santo, with eight.

Q   Who had the most triples in 1967?
A   Billy Williams, with 12.

Q   Who had the most triples in 1968?
A   Billy Williams, with eight.

Q   Who had the most triples in 1969?
A   Billy Williams, with 10.

Q   Did Robin Roberts ever pitch for the Cubs?
A   Yes. He finished his career in 1966 with Chicago winning two and losing three in eleven games.

Q   Within five points, what was Billy Williams' lifetime batting average?
A   .290

Q   Within 25, how many homeruns did Billy Williams hit in the major leagues?
A   426

Q   Robin Roberts closed out his career playing for the Chicago Cubs. Who got the last homerun surrendered by Roberts?
A   Willie Stargell of the Pittsburgh Pirates on September 3, 1966, got the last homerun, which was number 502, off the great Robin Roberts.

Q   Have any Chicago Cubs pitchers ever been named Fireman of the Year?
A   Yes, Lindy McDaniel in 1963; Ted Abernathy in 1965; Phil Regan (who spent part of the season with Los Angeles and finished with the Chicago Cubs) in 1968; Bruce Sutter in 1979; and Lee Smith in 1983 shared this honor with Al Holland of the Philadelphia Phillies.

Q   Did Ernie Banks ever play in the outfield?
A   Yes. He played in the outfield in 23 games in 1961.

Q   What was memorable about June 9, 1963?

A   Ernie Banks hit two homeruns off Sandy Koufax, and the Cubs lost to the Dodgers at Wrigley Field 11–8.

Q   Whom did the Cubs receive in a trade for Lou Brock?

A   They traded Lou, Jack Spring, and Paul Toth to St.Louis for Ernie Broglio, Bobby Shantz, and Doug Clemens on June 15, 1964, a day that will live in infamy.

Q   Ernie Banks had a long consecutive playing streak which ended on June 23, 1961. How many games had he played in?

A   717

Q   They had a day for Billy Williams on June 29, 1969. What did Billy do?

A   Billy had five hits as the Cubs defeated the Cardinals in a double-header.

Q   When did Billy Williams pass Stan Musial as the National Leaguers' all-time "iron man"?

A   Williams passed Musial by playing in his 895th and 896th consecutive games on June 29, 1969.

Q   What was memorable about the game on July 3, 1967?

A   There were five homeruns in the first inning, three by the Cubs and two by the Braves. Billy Williams, Ron Santo, and Randy Hundley hit for the Cubs, and Rico Carty and Felipe Alou for the Braves.

Q   Who hit pinch-hit homeruns in 1968?

A   Ernie Banks and Dick Nen

Q   Who hit pinch-hit homeruns in 1969?

A   Willie Smith (three times) and Jim Hickman

Q   What Cub players hit the most homeruns in the 1960's?

A   Ernie Banks had 269, Ron Santo had 253, and Billy Williams had 239, followed by George Altman with 71.

Q   Who led the Cubs in runs batted in in 1960?
A   Ernie Banks, with 117.

Q   Who led the Cubs in runs batted in in 1961?
A   George Altman, with 96.

Q   Who led the Cubs in runs batted in in 1962?
A   Ernie Banks, with 104.

Q   Who led the Cubs in runs batted in in 1963?
A   Ron Santo, with 99.

Q   Who led the Cubs in runs batted in in 1964?
A   Ron Santo, with 114.

Q   Who led the Cubs in runs batted in in 1965?
A   Billy Williams, with 108.

Q   Who led the Cubs in runs batted in in 1966?
A   Ron Santo, with 94.

Q   Who led the Cubs in runs batted in in 1967?
A   Ron Santo, with 98.

Q   Who led the Cubs in runs batted in in 1968?
A   Ron Santo and Billy Williams, both with 98.

Q   How many games did Ferguson Jenkins lose by the score of
     1–0 in 1968?
A   He lost five.

Q   Who was the youngest Cub to ever hit a homerun?
A   Danny Murphy, on September 13, 1960, at the age of 18
     years.

Q   What happened to Ken Holtzman on September 25, 1966?
A   Holtzman went to the ninth inning before allowing a hit. He gave up two but defeated Sandy Koufax for a 2–1 victory at Wrigley Field.

Q   When did Leo Durocher become manager of the Cubs?
A   On October 25, 1965.

Q   When did the Cubs decide that they would not have a manager, but would be run by a college of eight coaches?
A   In December of 1960.

Q   Who was the lading hitter for the Cubs in 1960?
A   Richie Ashburn, with .291.

Q   Who was the leading hitter for the Cubs in 1961?
A   George Altman, with .303.

Q   Who was the leading hitter for the Cubs in 1962?
A   George Altman, with .318.

Q   Who was the leading hitter for the Cubs in 1963?
A   Ron Santo, with .297.

Q   How did Ken Hubbs get killed?
A   Second baseman Ken Hubbs was killed in a plane crash near Provo, Utah, in February of 1964. It was his own plane.

Q   There has been only one nine-inning complete game in major league history in which there was only one hit. Where was it played?
A   It was played in Los Angeles September 9, 1965, between the Cubs and Los Angeles Dodgers.

Q   Who pitched the no-hitter on September 9, 1965?
A   Sandy Koufax pitched a perfect game as Los Angeles won 1–0.

Q   Who pitched for the Chicago Cubs?
A   Bob Hendley

Q   What player hit into a triple play on his final at-bat in his major league career?
A   On the final day of the 1962 season Joe Pignatano, who was catching for the New York Mets, hit into a triple play to end his major league career.

Q   When did Ernie Banks hit his 300th homerun?
A   Off Dick Farrell in Wrigley Field, April 18, 1962.

Q   When did Sandy Koufax strike out 18 batters?
A   On April 24, 1962, as the Dodgers tripped the Cubs 10–2. It was at Wrigley Field.

Q   When did Lou Boudreau take over as manager of the Cubs?
A   On May 4, 1960, Boudreau replaced Charlie Grimm as manager. Grimm, in turn, replaced Boudreau at the microphone.

Q   When did Barney Schultz win both ends of a double-header in relief against the Phillies?
A   On May 13, 1962.

Q   When did Ernie Banks drive in seven runs in one ballgame?
A   On May 13, 1969, against San Diego at Wrigley Field.

Q   What did Kenny Hubbs do on his big day?
A   On May 20, 1962, Ken collected eight hits in a double-header, going 3-for-3 in the first game and 5-for-5 in the second.

Q   When did Ernie Banks hit his final grand slam homerun?
A   On May 24, 1969, he hit his 12th and final grand slam as the Cubs beat the Padres 7–5 in San Diego.

Q   How did Ernie Banks do on his day at Wrigley Field?
A   They celebrated "Ernie Banks Day" on August 15, 1964, and Ernie failed to get the ball out of the infield. The Cubs lost to the Pirates 5–4.

Q   Did Jim Maloney ever pitch a no-hit game against the Cubs?
A   Yes. Maloney, pitching for Cincinnati, pitched a 10-inning no-hitter on August 19, 1965.

Q   Did Ken Holtzman ever pitch a no-hitter?
A   Ken pitched a no-hitter against the Braves on August 19, 1969, and one against the Reds, June 3, 1971, in Cincinnati.

Q   What did Cuno Barragan do on his first major league time at bat?
A   He hit a homerun against the Giants at Wrigley Field and never hit another homerun.

Q   Where did Ernie Banks hit his 400th homerun?
A   Ernie hit his 400th homerun off Bob Gibson at Wrigley Field on September 2, 1965.

Q   Kenny Hubbs broke Bobby Doerr's major league record for handling chances without an error at second base. When did this streak end?
A   On September 5, 1962, he made a wild throw against the Reds.

Q   When did Sandy Koufax pitch a perfect game against the Cubs?
A   On September 9, 1965.

Q   Future Cub pitcher Milt Pappas was traded by the Baltimore Orioles to the Cincinnati Reds in 1965. It was a trade Baltimore fans will never forget. Who did they receive in exchange for Pappas?
A   Frank Robinson went to Baltimore. Pappas came to the Cubs in 1968.

Q   Who led the Cubs in runs batted in in 1969?
A   Ron Santo, with 123.

Q   What Cub had the most stolen bases for one year in the 1960's?
A   Adolfo Phillips had 32 in 1966.

Q   What individual pitcher had the most victories for a Cub in the 1960's?
A   Larry Jackson had 24 in 1964.

Q   What Cub pitcher had the lowest earned run average in the 1960's?
A   Dick Ellsworth in 1963 had 2.11.

Q   What Cub pitcher had the most shutouts in any one season in the 1960's?
A   Ferguson Jenkins had seven shutouts in 1969.

Q   What Cub pitchers were named Fireman of the Year in the 1960's?
A   In 1963, Lindy McDaniel; in 1965, Ted Abernathy; and in 1968, Phil Regan.

Q   What Cub players were named Rookies of the Year in the 1960's?
A   Billy Williams in 1961, and Ken Hubbs in 1962.

Q   What Cub pitcher won the most games in 1960?
A   Glen Hobbie won 16.

Q   What Cub pitcher won the most games in 1961?
A   Don Cardwell won 15.

Q   What Cub pitcher won the most games in 1962?
A   Bob Buhl won 12.

Q What Cub pitcher won the most games in 1963?
A Dick Ellsworth won 22.

Q What Cub pitcher won the most games in 1964?
A Larry Jackson won 24.

Q What Cub pitcher won the most games in 1965?
A Dick Ellsworth and Larry Jackson won 14 each.

Q What Cub pitcher won the most games in 1966?
A Ken Holtzman won 11.

Q What Cub pitcher won the most games in 1967?
A Ferguson Jenkins won 20.

Q What Cub pitcher won the most games in 1968?
A Ferguson Jenkins won 20.

Q What Cub pitcher won the most games in 1969?
A Ferguson Jenkins won 21.

Q Where did Glenn Beckert go after the 1973 season?
A He went to San Diego with Bobby Fenwick in a trade for Jerry Morales.

Q What was Glenn Beckert's lifetime batting average?
A .283

Q How many runs did Glenn Beckert have in his 11 years in the Majors?
A 22

Q Joe Niekro spent 22 years in the Major Leagues. Did he ever pitch for the Cubs?
A Yes. He started his major league career with the Cubs in 1967 and stayed there until 1969 when he went to San Diego.

Q   Who won the National League pennant in 1960?
A   The Pittsburgh Pirates

Q   Who won the National League pennant in 1961?
A   The Cincinnati Reds

Q   Who won the National League pennant in 1962?
A   The San Francisco Giants

Q   Who won the pennant in the National League in 1963?
A   The Los Angeles Dodgers

Q   Who won the pennant in the National League in 1964?
A   The St. Louis Cardinals

Q   Who won the pennant in the National League in 1965?
A   The Los Angeles Dodgers

Q   Who won the pennant in the National League in 1966?
A   The Los Angeles Dodgers

Q   Who won the pennant in the National League in 1967?
A   The St. Louis Cardinals

Q   Who won the National League pennant in 1968?
A   The St. Louis Cardinals

Q   Who won the pennant in the National League in 1969?
A   The New York Mets

Q   Who won the batting crown in the National League in 1960?
A   Dick Groat, with .325.

Q   Who won the batting championship in the National League in 1961?
A   Roberto Clemente, with .351.

Q   Who won the batting championship in 1962?
A   Tommy Davis, with .346.

68

Q   Who won the batting championship in 1963?
A   Tommy Davis, with .326.

Q   Who won the National League batting crown in 1964?
A   Roberto Clemente, with .339.

Q   Who won the National League batting championship in 1965?
A   Roberto Clemente, with .329.

Q   Who won the batting crown in the National League in 1966?
A   Matty Aloo, with .342.

Q   Who won the batting title in the National League in 1967?
A   Roberto Clemente, with .357.

Q   Who won the batting title in the National League in 1968?
A   Pete Rose, with .335.

Q   Who won the batting championship in the National League in 1969?
A   Pete Rose, with .348.

CHAPTER FOUR
THE CHICAGO CUBS
IN THE 1970'S

Q   Who was the last batter to get a hit off Bob Gibson?
A   Pete LaCock pinch-hitted when playing for Chicago against the Cardinals September 3, 1975, and doubled off Gibson, the last hit Gibson was ever going to give up.

Q   In 1976 two idiots tried to set afire the United States flag in the outfield of Dodger Stadium. Who was the Cub outfielder who rescued the flag?
A   Rick Monday

Q   How did the Cubs get Bill Madlock?
A   The Cubs traded Bobby Mercer, Steve Ontiveros, and Andy Mulstock on February 11, 1977, to the Giants for Madlock and Bob Sperring.

Q   Who did Ernie Banks hit his 500th homerun off of?
A   Pat Jarvis of the Atlanta Braves on May 12, 1970.

Q   The Cubs traded Billy Williams to Oakland in 1974. Whom did they get in exchange?
A   Bob Locker, Manny Trillo, and Darold Knowles.

Q   What Pittsburgh ballplayer got seven hits in one game against the Cubs?
A   Rennie Stennett, September 16, 1975, went 7-for-7 as the Pirates beat the Cubs 22–0.

Q   What Cub led the team in two base hits in 1972?
A   Billy Williams, with 34.

Q   What Cub led the team in two base hits in 1973?
A   Jose Cardenal, with 33.

Q   What Cub led the team in two base hits in 1974?
A   Jose Cardenal, with 35.

Q   What Cub led the team in two base hits in 1975?
A   Jose Cardenal, with 30.

Q   What Cub led the team in two base hits in 1976?
A   Bill Madlock, with 36.

Q   What Cub led the team in two base hits in 1977?
A   Jerry Morales, with 34.

Q   What Cub led the team in two base hits in 1978?
A   Bill Buckner, with 26.

Q   What Cub led the team in two base hits in 1979?
A   Bill Buckner and Jerry Martin, with 34 each.

Q   How many times did Ferguson Jenkins win 20 games in a season?
A   On seven different occasions, from 1967 through 1972, for the Cubs. He also won 25 for Texas in 1974.

Q   How did the Cubs obtain Ferguson Jenkins?
A   The Cubs traded Adolfo Phillips, Jenkins, and John Herrnstein for Larry Jackson and Bob Buhl.

72

Q Did Rich Reuschel ever win 20 games for the Cubs?
A Yes. In 1977 he won 20 and lost 10.

Q Is Ralph Kiner in baseball's Hall of Fame?
A Yes. He was elected in 1975.

Q Who was the first all-brother shutout?
A Rich and Paul Reuschel combined to pitch a shutout as the Cubs beat the Dodgers 7–0 in 1975 on August 21.

Q Did Ron Santo ever get more than 2,000 hits?
A Yes. On August 26, 1972, Ron got his 2,000th hit, which was a three-run homer at Wrigley Field against the Giants.

Q How long did Ron Santo play for the Cubs?
A Santo played 14 years. He came up in 1960 and played through 1973.

Q Has a pitcher ever pitched a perfect game for the Cubs?
A No, but Milt Pappas missed a perfect game when he walked Larry Stall on a 3–2 pitch with two outs in the ninth inning of a game with the San Diego Padres on September 2, 1972. Stall was the only man to reach first base.

Q When did Milt Pappas play for the Cubs?
A Milt Pappas played for the Cubs in 1970, 1971, 1972, and 1973.

Q How many years did Milt Pappas pitch in the major leagues?
A 17 years

Q Robin Roberts, who pitched in the major leagues for 19 years mainly with the Philadelphia Phillies, later went to Baltimore, Houston, and then to the Cubs. Is he in the Hall of Fame?
A Yes. He was elected to baseball's Hall of Fame in 1976.

73

Q   What was the opening day lineup in 1975?
A   D. Kessinger, shortstop; J. Cardenal, left field; B. Madlock, third base; R. Monday, centerfield; J. Morales, right field; P. LaCock, first base; M. Trillo, second base; S. Swisher, catcher; B. Bonham, pitcher.

Q   What was the opening day lineup in 1976?
A   R. Monday, centerfield; J. Cardenal, left field; B. Madlock, third base; J. Morales, right field; A. Thornton, first base; M. Trillo, second base; S. Swisher, catcher; D. Rosello, shortstop; R. Burris, pitcher.

Q   What was the opening day lineup in 1977?
A   I. DeJesus, shortstop; J. Cardenal, left field; L. Biitner, first base; B. Murcer, right field; J. Morales, centerfield; S. Ontiveros, third base; S. Swisher, catcher; M. Trillo, second base; R. Burris, pitcher.

Q   What was the opening day lineup in 1978?
A   I. DeJesus, shortstop; G. Gross, centerfield; B. Buckner, first base; B. Murcer, right field; D. Kingman, left field; S. Ontiveros, third base; M. Trillo, second base; D. Rader, catcher; R. Reuschel, pitcher.

Q   What was the opening day lineup in 1979?
A   I. DeJesus, shortstop; T. Sizemore, second base; B. Buckner, first base; D. Kingman, left field; B. Murcer, right field; S. Ontiveros, third base; J. Martin, centerfield; B. Foote, catcher; R. Reuschel, pitcher.

Q   In what years did the Cubs operate without a manager, but instead with a group of men called the College of Coaches?
A   In 1961 and 1962

Q   Who were the College of Coaches?
A   In 1961 and 1962, they were Vedie Himsel, Harry Craft, Lou Klein, and Elvin Tappe.

74

Q   Who were the coaches who managed the club in 1962?
A   There were three: Elvin Tappe, Charlie Metro, and Lou Klein.

Q   How many Cubs were named to the All Star team in 1969?
A   A record breaking five: Ernie Banks, Glen Beckert, Randy Hundley, Don Kessinger, and Ron Santo.

Q   Did any Cub pitchers win 20 or more games in the 1960's besides Ferguson Jenkins?
A   Larry Jackson won 24 and lost 11 in 1964, Bill Hands won 20 games in 1969, and Dick Ellsworth won 20 games in 1963.

Q   How many years in a row did Ferguson Jenkins win 20 games?
A   Six. He started in 1967 and won 20 or more games every year until 1973.

Q   What Cubs were named to the All Star team in 1970?
A   Glen Beckert, Jim Hickman, and Don Kessinger.

Q   What Cubs were named to the All Star team in 1971?
A   Glen Beckert, Ferguson Jenkins, Don Kessinger, and Ron Santo.

Q   What Cubs were named to the All Star team in 1972?
A   Glen Beckert, Ferguson Jenkins, Don Kessinger, Ron Santo, and Billy Williams.

Q   What Cubs were named to the All Star team in 1973?
A   Ron Santo and Billy Williams

Q   What Cubs were named to the All Star team in 1974?
A   Don Kessinger

Q   What Cubs were named to the All Star team in 1975?
A   Bill Madlock

Q   What Cubs were named to the All Star team in 1976?
A   Steve Swisher

Q   What Cubs were named to the All Star team in 1977?
A   Jerry Morales, Rick Reuschel, Bruce Sutter, and Manny Trillo.

Q   What Cubs were named to the All Star team in 1978?
A   Bruce Sutter

Q   What Cubs were named to the All Star team in 1979?
A   Dave Kingman and Bruce Sutter

Q   Did Billy Williams ever lead the National League in batting?
A   Yes, in 1972.

Q   Was Billy Williams ever named Major League Player of the Year by *The Sporting News*?
A   Yes, in 1972.

Q   Did Don Zimmer ever manage a major league baseball team before managing the Cubs?
A   Yes. He managed the Padres from 1972 through 1973, the Red Sox from 1976 through 1980, and the Texas Rangers in 1981 and 1982.

Q   In how many consecutive games did Billy Williams play?
A   He played in 1,117 from 1961 to 1974.

Q   In 1973 the Cubs traded the great Ferguson Jenkins to Texas. Whom did they get in exchange?
A   Vic Harris and Bill Madlock

Q   Has any Cub ever gotten six hits in one ballgame?
A   In the modern era, Don Kessinger, in 1971; Bill Madlock, in 1975; and Jose Cardenal, in 1976.

Q Who was the first Chicago Cub pitcher to be named Pitcher of the Year?
A Ferguson Jenkins in 1971

Q In the All Star Game in Cincinnati in 1970, Pete Rose barrelled into Gary Fosse and scored the winning run. What Cub player got the hit that scored Rose?
A Jim Hickman

Q When Pete Rose started his 44-game hitting streak, who was the pitcher that gave up the first hits?
A Dave Roberts of the Chicago Cubs

Q When did Pete start his streak?
A June 14, 1978

Q Who led the Cubs in runs batted in in 1971?
A Billy Williams, with 93.

Q Who led the Cubs in runs batted in in 1972?
A Billy Williams, with 122.

Q Who led the Cubs in runs batted in in 1973?
A Billy Williams, with 86.

Q Who led the Cubs in runs batted in in 1974?
A Jerry Morales, with 82.

Q Who led the Cubs in runs batted in in 1975?
A Jerry Morales, with 91.

Q Who led the Cubs in runs batted in in 1976?
A Bill Madlock, with 84.

Q Who led the Cubs in runs batted in in 1977?
A Bobby Murcer, with 89.

Q   Who led the Cubs in runs batted in in 1978?
A   Dave Kingman, with 79.

Q   Who led the Cubs in runs batted in in 1979?
A   Dave Kingman, with 115.

Q   Who led the Cubs in homeruns in 1970?
A   Billy Williams, with 42.

Q   Who led the Cubs in homeruns in 1971?
A   Billy Williams, with 28.

Q   Who led the Cubs in homeruns in 1972?
A   Billy Williams, with 37.

Q   Who led the Cubs in homeruns in 1973?
A   Rick Monday, with 26.

Q   On August 22, 1970 Ken Holtzman went to the eighth inning before allowing a hit. Who got the hit?
A   Hal Lanier of San Francisco in San Francisco

Q   When did Ernie Banks hit his last homerun?
A   Banks hit his 512th and final homerun on August 24, 1971.

Q   On August 26, 1972, Ron Santo hit a three-run homerun as the Cubs beat the Giants 10-9 at Wrigley Field. What was outstanding about the hit?
A   It was his 3,000th career hit.

Q   When did Billy Williams' streak of playing in 1,170 consecutive games end?
A   On September 3, 1970, he did not play.

Q   When did Ron Santo hit his 300th homer and where did he hit it?
A   On September 21, 1971, at Wrigley Field.

Q   How many games did Ernie Banks play in and when did his career end?

A   On September 26, Banks played his last game (his 2,528th) at Wrigley Field.

Q   When did Gabby Hartnett die?

A   December 20, 1972, at the age of 72.

Q   Glen Beckert hit safely in how many straight games in 1973?

A   Beckert hit in 26 games. His streak was broken on May 18.

Q   When did Ken Holtzman pitch his second no-hitter?

A   June 3, 1971, at Riverfront Stadium in Cincinnati. He also scored the only run of the game.

Q   Who spoiled Dennis Lamp's try for a no-hitter on June 9, 1978?

A   Gene Richards got a single with two outs in the sixth as the Cubs beat San Diego 5-0.

Q   When did Don Kessinger get 6 hits in as many times at bat?

A   On June 17, 1971, as Chicago beat the Cardinals 7-6 at Wrigley Field.

Q   When did Rick Reuschel make his first major league start?

A   On June 26, 1972, Reuschel beat the Phillies 11-1 at Wrigley Field.

Q   When did Whitey Lockman replace Leo Durocher as Cub manager?

A   July 24, 1972

Q   When was Whitey Lockman replaced as manager by Jim Marshall?

A   July 24, 1974

Q   Did Bill Madlock ever have 6 hits in one game?

A   Yes. On July 26, 1975 Bill had five singles and a triple.

79

Q   Who led the Cubs in batting in 1970?
A   Billy Williams, with .322.

Q   Who led the Cubs in batting in 1971?
A   Glen Beckert, with .342.

Q   Who led the Cubs in batting in 1973?
A   Jose Cardenal, with .303.

Q   Who led the Cubs in batting in 1974?
A   Bill Madlock, with .313.

Q   Who led the Cubs in batting in 1975?
A   Bill Madlock, with .354. He also led the major leagues in hitting.

Q   Who led the Cubs in batting in 1976?
A   Bill Madlock, with .339. He also led the major leagues in hitting.

Q   Who led the Cubs in batting in 1977?
A   Steve Ontiveros, with .299.

Q   Who led the Cubs in batting in 1978?
A   Bill Buckner, with .323.

Q   Who led the Cubs in batting in 1979?
A   Scott Thompson, with .289.

Q   Who led the Cubs in runs batted in in 1970?
A   Billy Williams, with 129.

Q   When did Phil Wrigley die?
A   Wrigley died at the age of 82 on April 12, 1977.

Q   Did Bert Hooton ever pitch a no-hitter?
A   Yes, in 1972 on April 16 at Wrigley Field, beating the Phillies 4–0.

Q   When Schmidt hit four consecutive homeruns, where was the game played?

A   Schmidt hit four consecutive homeruns against the Cubs on April 17, 1976, at Wrigley Field.

Q   What was the longest hitting streak of Glen Beckert's career?

A   Beckert hit in 26 straight games in 1973.

Q   Who broke the potential no-hitter of Dennis Lamp?

A   Gene Richards of the Padres with a single in the sixth on June 9, 1978.

Q   Was Bruce Sutter ever credited with a win in an All Star game?

A   Yes. In 1978 he retired all five batters he faced and gained the credit for the victory, 7–3, at San Diego.

Q   When did Bruce Sutter win his second game in an All Star game?

A   July 18, 1979

Q   What was the opening day lineup in 1970?

A   D. Kessinger, shortstop; G. Beckert, second base; B. Williams, left field; R. Santo, third base; E. Banks, first base; J. Callison, rightfield; J. Hickman, centerfield; J. C. Martin, Catcher; F. Jenkins, pitcher.

Q   What was the opening day lineup in 1971?

A   D. Kessinger, shortstop; G. Beckert, second base; B. Williams, leftfield; R. Santo, third base; J. Pepitone, first base; J. Callison, rightfield; J. Ortiz, centerfield; K. Rudolph, catcher; F. Jenkins, pitcher.

Q   What was the opening day lineup in 1972?

A   J. Cardenal, rightfield; G. Beckert, second base; R. Santo, third base; J. Pepitone, first base; R. Hundley, catcher; R. Monday, centerfield; D. Kessinger, shortstop; F. Jenkins, pitcher.

Q   What was the opening day lineup in 1973?
A   R. Monday, centerfield; J. Cardenal, rightfield; B. Williams, leftfield; J. Pepitone, first base; R. Santo, third base; G. Beckert, second base; R. Hundley, catcher; D. Kessinger, shortstop; F. Jenkins, pitcher.

Q   What was the opening day lineup in 1974?
A   V. Harris, second base; R. Monday, centerfield; J. Morales, leftfield; B. Williams, first base; J. Cardenal, rightfield; B. Madlock, third base; G. Mitterwald, catcher; D. Kessinger, shortstop; B. Bonham, pitcher.

Q   What Cub pitcher won the most games in 1971?
A   Ferguson Jenkins, with 24.

Q   What Cub pitcher won the most games in 1972?
A   Ferguson Jenkins, with 20.

Q   What Cub pitcher won the most games in 1973?
A   Rick Reuschel, Ferguson Jenkins, and Bert Hooten all were tied with 14.

Q   What Cub pitcher won the most games in 1974?
A   Rick Reuschel, with 13.

Q   What Cub pitcher won the most games in 1975?
A   Ray Burris, with 15.

Q   What Cub pitcher won the most games in 1976?
A   Ray Burris, with 15.

Q   What Cub pitcher won the most games in 1977?
A   Rick Reuschel, with 20.

Q   What Cub pitcher won the most games in 1978?
A   Rick Reuschel, with 14.

Q   What Cub pitcher won the most games in 1979?
A   Rick Reuschel, with 18.

Q   How many strikeouts did Ferguson Jenkins have in his career?
A   From 1966 to 1973 he had 1,808 strikeouts.

Q   How long did Randy Hundley play for the Cubs?
A   He joined the Cubs in 1966 and played through the 1973 season, went to Minnesota, came back to the Cubs in 1976, and finished his career in 1977.

Q   What was Randy Hundley's lifetime batting average?
A   .236

Q   Off what team did Lou Brock collect his 3,000th hit when he was playing for the Cardinals?
A   On August 13, 1979, he hit number 3,000 against the Cubs.

Q   How long did Kenny Holtzman pitch for the Cubs?
A   Holtzman had two terms with the Cubs. He started out in 1965, and stayed until 1971. He came back to the Cubs in 1978.

Q   What was Holtzman's best year?
A   His best year with the Cubs was in 1970 when he won 17 games and lost 11.

Q   When did Ken Holtzman leave the Cubs?
A   He was traded in November 1971 to Oakland for Rick Monday.

Q   Who was the last pitcher to hit a homerun in the World Series?
A   Ken Holtzman, when he was with Oakland in 1974.

Q   Who did Lou Brock collect his 3,000th hit off of?

A   Lou Brock, who is a former Cub, got his 3,000th hit against the Cubs on August 13, 1979.

Q   Have any Cub announcers been given the Ford Frick Award for their broadcasting by the Hall of Fame?

A   Yes. Bob Elson in 1979, Jack Brickhouse in 1983, and Harry Caray in 1989.

Q   Has the J.G. Taylor Spink Award ever been given to any of the Chicago sportswriters?

A   Yes. "Ring" Lardner, Charles Dryden, Warren Brown, John Carmichael, and Ed Munsel.

Q   How did the Cubs get Bill Buckner?

A   Bill Buckner, Ivan DeJesus, and Jeff Albert came to the Cubs in a trade for Rick Monday and Mike Garman in January of 1977.

Q   What Chicago Cub pitchers have won the Cy Young Award?

A   Three: Ferguson Jenkins, 1971; Bruce Sutter, 1979; and Rick Sutcliffe, 1984.

Q   What was the greatest number of games that Milt Pappas won during his career with the Cubs?

A   17 (in 1971 and again in 1972)

Q   Which Cub pitcher had the most shutouts in 1970?

A   Ferguson Jenkins, with three.

Q   Which Cub pitcher had the most shutouts in 1971?

A   Milt Pappas, with five.

Q   Which Cub pitcher had the most shutouts in 1972?

A   Ferguson Jenkins, with five.

Q   Which Cub pitcher had the most shutouts in 1973?

A   Rick Reuschel, with three.

Q   Which Cub pitcher had the most shutouts in 1974?
A   Rich Reuschel and Bonham, with two each.

Q   Which Cub pitcher had the most shutouts in 1975?
A   Ray Burris and Bill Bonham, with two each.

Q   Which Cub pitcher had the most shutouts in 1976?
A   Ray Burris

Q   Which Cub pitcher had the most shutouts in 1977?
A   Rich Reuschel, with four.

Q   Which Cub pitcher had the most shutouts in 1978?
A   Rich Reuschel, with three.

Q   Which Cub pitcher had the most shutouts in 1979?
A   Ken Holtzman, with two.

Q   What Cub pitcher had the most wins in the 1970's?
A   Rick Reuschel won 114 and lost 101.

Q   What Cub pitcher had the most consecutive victories in the 1970's?
A   Milt Pappas won 11 in a row in 1972.

Q   What Cub pitcher won the most games in 1970?
A   Ferguson Jenkins, with 22.

Q   What years was Jim Marshall the pilot for the Chicago Cubs?
A   Part of 1974, all of 1975 and 1976.

Q   When did Herman Franks manage the Cubs?
A   In 1977, 1978, and part of 1979.

Q   Who won the pennant in the National League in 1970?
A   The Cincinnati Reds

Q   Who won the National League pennant in 1971?
A   The Pittsburgh Pirates

Q   Who won the National League pennant in 1972?
A   The Cincinnati Reds

Q   Who won the National League pennant in 1973?
A   The New York Mets

Q   Who won the National League pennant in 1974?
A   The Los Angeles Dodgers

Q   Who won the National League pennant in 1975?
A   The Cincinnati Reds

Q   Who won the National League in 1976?
A   The Cincinnati Reds

Q   Who won the National League pennant in 1977?
A   The Los Angeles Dodgers

Q   Who won the National League pennant in 1978?
A   The Los Angeles Dodgers

Q   Who won the National League pennant in 1979?
A   The Pittsburgh Pirates

Q   Who won the National League batting championship in 1970?
A   Ricardo Carty, who hit .366.

Q   Who won the National League batting title in 1971?
A   Joe Torre, who hit .363.

Q   Who won the National League batting crown in 1972?
A   Billy Williams, who hit .333.

Q   Who won the National League batting championship in 1973?
A   Pete Rose with .338.

Q   Who won the National League batting championship in 1979?
A   Keith Hernandez, with .344.

Q   Who won the National League batting crown in 1978?
A   Dave Parker, with .334.

Q   Who won the batting championship in 1977?
A   Dave Parker, with .338.

Q   Who won the championship batting title in the National League in 1974?
A   Ralph Garr, who hit .353.

Q   Who won the batting championship in the National League in 1975?
A   Bill Madlock, with .354.

Q   Who won the batting title in the National League in 1976?
A   Bill Madlock, with .339.

CHAPTER FIVE
THE CHICAGO CUBS
IN THE 1980'S

Q   Who were the umpires for the first game of the Champion-
     ship Series in 1984?
A   A strike by major league umpires caused the leagues to call in
     college and former pro umpires to work the games.

Q   Who won the second game of the Championship Series in
     1984?
A   The Cubs won 4-2. "Rainbow" Trout scattered five hits and
     Lee Smith came in in the ninth inning to get the last two outs.
     The final score was 4-2.

Q   Who won the third game of the Championship Series in
     1984?
A   Beating Dennis Eckersley the San Diego Padres won 7-1.

Q   Who won the fourth game of the Championship Series in
     1984?
A   San Diego won 7-5. Steve Garvey had four hits in five times
     at bat and drove in five runs. It was one of the most dramatic
     games ever played as San Diego scored two in the ninth to
     win.

Q   Who won the last game of the Championship Series in 1984?

A   San Diego won 6–3 with Rick Sutcliffe taking the loss. Leon Durham's error allowed Martinez to score the tying run and then three straight singles capped the four run rally that won the game.

Q   In the 1984 Championship Series what Cubs hit homeruns?

A   Leon Durham had two and so did Jody Davis and Gary Matthews. Rich Sutcliffe also had one, as did Bob Dernier and Ron Cey.

Q   Who was the leading hitter for the Cubs in the Championship Series in 1984?

A   Jody Davis hit .389 and Ron Sandberg hit .368. Keith Moreland hit .333.

Q   What former Cub who played in 1984 was a grave digger in the off-season?

A   Richie Hebner, during the off-season at a cemetery where his father is a foreman.

Q   When was the first night game played at Wrigley Field?

A   On August 8, 1988.

Q   When were the Chicago Cubs sold to the Tribune Company?

A   1981

Q   How long has Harry Carey been announcing the games?

A   Carey marked in his 46th season of broadcasting major league baseball in 1990; this was his eighth with the Cubs. Carey was the voice of the White Sox for 11 years before joining the Cubs broadcasting team in 1982. He previously had spent 25 years broadcasting St. Louis Cardinal games and one season announcing the Oakland Athletic games.

Q How long has Steve Stone been broadcasting with Harry Carey?

A Stone retired from baseball in June 1982 after suffering an arm injury. He will be in his seventh year with WGN.

Q What is the most number of runs batted in Andre Dawson ever had in one year?

A Dawson led the National League in batting with 137 in 1987.

Q When did Rick Reuschel pitch for the Cubs?

A Rich was with the Cubs from 1972 to 1981, then went to the Yankees and came back to the Cubs in 1983, staying until 1985.

Q Who did the Cubs trade Rick Reuschel for in 1981?

A He was traded to the New York Yankees for Doug Bird, Mike Griffin, and cash.

Q How long was Lee Smith with the Cubs?

A Lee joined the Cubs in 1980 and stayed with them through 1987.

Q Did Lee Smith ever start a ballgame or did he always pitch strictly relief?

A He started six games, one in 1981 and one in 1982.

Q Did Lee Smith ever lead the National League in number of saves?

A Yes, in 1983 with 29 saves.

Q Whom did the Cubs trade Lee Smith for?

A He was traded to the Boston Red Sox for Al Nipper and Calvin Schiraldi in December 1987.

Q Who had the most saves lifetime as a Cub pitcher?

A Lee Smith, with 180.

Q   The Cubs had two managers in 1980. Who were they?
A   Preston Gomez and Joey Amalfitano

Q   Did Charlie Fox ever pilot the Cubs?
A   Yes, for 39 games in 1983.

Q   What were the years that Lee Elia was the skipper for the Cubs?
A   1982 and 1983

Q   Jimmy Frey, now the General Manager of the cubs, piloted them on the field in what years?
A   1984, 1985, and part of 1986.

Q   Did Gene Michael ever manage the Cubs?
A   Yes, during part of 1986 and 1987.

Q   How long has Don Zimmer been managing the Cubs?
A   Don took over in 1988.

Q   Who were Cub coaches in 1984?
A   Billy Connors, Ruben Amaro, Johnny Oates, Don Zimmer, and John Vukovich.

Q   How did the Cubs get ahold of Andre Dawson?
A   Dawson was signed as a free agent on March 6, 1987.

Q   What is the most number of homeruns Andre Dawson ever hit?
A   Dawson hit 49 homeruns in 1987 to lead the National League.

Q   In 1984 the Cubs won the Eastern Championship of the National League. Give their infield.
A   First base was Leon Durham, second base was Ryne Sandberg, Ron Cey was at third, and Larry Bowa was at short.

Q   Give the outfield of the Cubs in 1984.

A   Keith Moreland, Bobby Dernier, and Gary Matthews.

Q   What catcher caught the most games with the Championship Cubs in 1984?

A   Jody Davis

Q   Was Ryne Sandberg ever named Player of the Year?

A   Yes, in 1984.

Q   Was Rick Sutcliffe ever named Pitcher of the Year?

A   Yes, in 1984 and 1987.

Q   Pete Rose's 4,191 career hit, which tied him with Ty Cobb for most hits in baseball, was made at Wrigley Field. Who did he get the hit off?

A   Reggie Patterson on September 8, 1985.

Q   Who were the Cub members who were chosen for the All Star team in 1988?

A   Andre Dawson, Shawon Dunston, Vance Law, Greg Maddux, Rafael Palmeiro, and Ryne Sandberg.

Q   What position did the Cubs finish in in 1980?

A   Sixth

Q   What position did the Cubs finish in in 1981?

A   Sixth

Q   What position did the Cubs finish in in 1982?

A   Fifth

Q   What position did the Cubs finish in in 1983?

A   Fifth

Q   What position did the Cubs finish in in 1984?

A   First

Q   What position did the Cubs finish in in 1985?
A   Fourth

Q   What position did the Cubs finish in in 1986?
A   Fifth

Q   What position did the Cubs finish in in 1987?
A   Sixth

Q   What position did the Cubs finish in in 1988?
A   Fourth

Q   What position did the Cubs finish in in 1989?
A   First

Q   Who led the Cubs in homeruns in 1980?
A   Jerry Martin, with 23.

Q   Who led the Cubs in homeruns in 1981?
A   Bill Buckner and "Bull" Durham, with 10 each.

Q   Who led the Cubs in homeruns in 1982?
A   "Bull" Durham, with 22.

Q   Who led the Cubs in homeruns in 1983?
A   Ron Cey and Jody Davis, with 24.

Q   Who led the Cubs in homeruns in 1984?
A   Ron Cey, with 25.

Q   Who led the Cubs in homeruns in 1985?
A   Ryne Sandberg, with 26.

Q   Who led the Cubs in homeruns in 1986?
A   Gary Matthews and Jody Davis, with 21 each.

Q   Who led the Cubs in homeruns in 1987?
A   Andre Dawson, with 49.

Q   Who led the Cubs in homeruns in 1988?
A   Andre Dawson

Q   Who led the Cubs in homeruns in 1989?
A   Ryne Sandberg, with 30.

Q   What is the Cub record for a pitcher winning most consecutive games?
A   Ed Reulbach and Rick Sutcliffe each have won 14 games in a row.

Q   Who was the Cub RBI leader in 1980?
A   Jerry Martin, with 73.

Q   Who was the Cub RBI leader in 1981?
A   Bill Buckner, with 75.

Q   Who was the Cub RBI leader in 1982?
A   Bill Buckner, with 105.

Q   Who was the Cub RBI leader in 1983?
A   Ron Cey, with 90.

Q   Who was the Cub RBI leader in 1984?
A   Ron Cey, with 97.

Q   Who was the Cub RBI leader in 1985?
A   Keith Moreland, with 106.

Q   Who was the Cub RBI leader in 1986?
A   Keith Moreland, with 79.

Q   Who was the Cub RBI leader in 1987?
A   Andre Dawson, with 137.

Q   Who was the Cub RBI leader in 1988?
A   Andre Dawson, with 79.

Q   Who was the Cub RBI leader in 1989?

A   Mark Grace with 79, beating Andre Dawson by two and Ryne Sandberg by three.

Q   What was the Chicago Cubs team batting average for 1989?

A   They led the League with a .261 average.

Q   Who led the Cubs in triples in 1989?

A   Dave Smith, Shawon Dunston, and Andre Dawson had six each.

Q   Who led the Cubs in two base hits in 1989?

A   Mark Grace had 28.

Q   Mitch Williams had 36 saves for the Cubs in 1989, which was the highest of any member of the pitching staff. Who was second?

A   Les Lancaster, who had eight.

Q   Who did Mark Grace hit his first homerun off?

A   Off a left-hander named Keith Comstock of San Diego.

Q   Who was the National League Rookie of the Year in 1988?

A   Mark Grace

Q   In 1987 Mark Grace played in the Eastern League with Pittsfield. What was his batting average?

A   .333

Q   Who was the Most Valuable Player in the Eastern League in 1987?

A   Mark Grace

Q   Where did Mark Grace go to college

A   Saddleback College in Mission Viejo, California.

Q   In 1988 Mark Grace hit seven homeruns for the Cubs. How many were on the road?
A   All seven.

Q   Who were the coaches for the 1989 Cubs?
A   Joe Altobelli, Chick Cottier, Larry Cox, Jose Martinez, and Dick Pole.

Q   What Cubs have hit for the cycle in the 1980's?
A   Andre Dawson in April 1987; Ivan DeJesus hit for the cycle in 1980.

Q   How many complete games did Les Lancaster have in 1988?
A   One. He started 18 games.

Q   Who was the youngest Cub to ever to to an All Star game?
A   Greg Maddux

Q   In 1987, who was the youngest player in the League?
A   Greg Maddux. He was 20 years old at the start of the season.

Q   Did Greg Maddux ever pitch against his brother Mike?
A   Yes. He beat his brother Mike in a game on September 29, 1988.

Q   How did the Cubs secure Greg Maddux?
A   He was selected by the Cubs in the second round draft of June 1984.

Q   What is Greg Maddux's longest winning streak?
A   Nine games: from May 22 to October 7, 1988.

Q   Whom did Ryne Sandberg hit his 100th Major League homerun off?
A   Neal Heaton on June 19, 1988.

Q   "Wild Fire" Schulte stole 57 bases in 1906. What is the second highest number ever stolen by a Cub?

A   Ryne Sandberg stole 54 in 1985.

Q   What is the highest batting average Ryne Sandberg has had since joining the Cubs?

A   He hit .314 in 1984.

Q   What is the greatest number of runs batted in by Ryne Sandberg since he joined the Cubs?

A   He batted in 84 in 1984.

Q   In 1984 Ryne Sandberg tied for the League in triples. How many did he have?

A   19

Q   What was Ryne Sandberg's first year with the Cubs?

A   1982

Q   How long was Ryne Sandberg in the Minors before he came up to Philadelphia?

A   Four years

Q   How did the Cubs obtain Ryne Sandberg?

A   He came with Larry Bowa in exchange for Ivan DeJesus.

Q   What was the most victories that Scott Sanderson has ever had?

A   He won 16 and lost 11 in 1980, pitching for Montreal.

Q   When did the Cubs get Scott Sanderson?

A   He came in a three-team trade from Montreal in December 1983.

Q   Did Scott Sanderson ever hit a homerun?

A   Yes. His first career homerun was a grand slam off the Cubs' Randy Martz at Wrigley Field in September 1982. He was pitching for Montreal then.

Q   How did the Cubs get Calvin Schiraldi?
A   Schiraldi came to the Cubs with pitcher Al Nipper in exchange for Lee Smith on December 8, 1987.

Q   How did the Cubs get Dwight Smith?
A   He was selected by the Cubs in the third round, secondary phase of the June draft in 1984.

Q   Who were the Cub members who were chosen for the All Star team in 1980?
A   Dave Kingman and Bruce Sutter

Q   Who was the Cub member who was chosen for the All Star team in 1981?
A   Bill Buckner

Q   Who was the Cub member who was chosen for the All Star team in 1982?
A   "Bull" Durham

Q   Who were the Cub members who were chosen for the All Star team in 1983?
A   "Bull" Durham and Lee Smith

Q   Who were the Cub members who were chosen for the All Star team in 1984?
A   Jody Davis and Ryne Sandberg

Q   Who was the Cub member who was chosen for the All Star team in 1985?
A   Ryne Sandberg

Q   Who were the Cub members who were chosen for the All Star team in 1986?
A   Jody Davis and Ryne Sandberg

Q   Who were the Cub members who were chosen for the All Star team in 1987?

A   Andre Dawson, Ryne Sandberg, Lee Smith, and Rich Sutcliffe.

Q   What Cubs won the Gold Glove Award in 1986?

A   Ryne Sandberg and Jody Davis

Q   What Cubs won the Gold Glove Award in 1987?

A   Ryne Sandberg and Andre Dawson

Q   What Cubs won the Gold Glove Award in 1988?

A   Ryne Sandberg and Andre Dawson

Q   Who was the last Cub pitcher to steal home?

A   On July 29, 1988, Rick Sutcliffe stole home in the seventh inning at Philadelphia.

Q   Whom did the Cubs receive in exchange for Jody Davis?

A   Kevin Blankenship and Kevin Coffman

Q   How did the Cubs obtain Mitch Webster?

A   In a trade for Dave Martinez on July 14, 1988.

Q   Whom did the Cubs obtain in trade for "Bull" Durham?

A   Durham was traded to Cincinnati for Pat Perry on May 19, 1988.

Q   Who was the first Cub to ever have his uniform retired?

A   Ernie Banks on August 22, 1982.

Q   When did the Cubs play their longest game in history?

A   July 6, 1980. It was 5 1/2 hours and 20 innings.

Q   Where was the longest game in Cubs history played?

A   Three River Stadium in Pittsburgh.

100

Q   When was Preston Gomez relieved as Manager and who took his place?
A   July 25, 1980; Joe Amalfitano replaced Gomez.

Q   On September 10, 1980, 18 Cubs were struck out in a game with the Expos. Who was pitching for Montreal?
A   Bill Gullickson. It was his first year in the Majors.

Q   When was Lee Elia named Manager of the Cubs?
A   October 22, 1981, Elia replaced Amalfitano.

Q   What Cubs have hit over .300 in the 1980's?
A   Bill Buckner hit .324 in 1980 and .311 in 1981.

Q   How did the Cubs obtain the services of Jerome Walton?
A   He was selected by the Cubs in the second round of the 1986 January draft.

Q   How many years did Jerome Walton spend in the Minor Leagues before coming p to the Cubs?
A   Three

Q   How long was Mitch Williams with the Texas Rangers before coming to the Cubs?
A   Three years. He started in 1986.

Q   What was Mitch Williams' best record with Texas?
A   He won eight and lost six in both 1986 and 1987.

Q   The Cubs won the division championship in 1989. Where did they finish in 1988?
A   Fourth

Q   How many games were the Cubs behind the first place club in the east division in 1988?
A   24

Q   What Cub had the most homeruns in any one month since 1900?

A   Andre Dawson had 15 homeruns in August of 1987.

Q   What Cubs pinch-hitted the most homeruns in any one season?

A   Willie Smith and Thad Bosley each did it three times.

Q   How long did Keith Moreland play with the Cubs?

A   Keith was with the Cubs from 1982 through 1987.

Q   How long was Gary Matthews with the Cubs?

A   Matthews came to the Cubs in 1984 and stayed there until 1987.

Q   What was Mark Grace's batting average in the playoffs in 1989?

A   .640

Q   How did the Cubs get Mike Bielecki?

A   He came to the Cubs in a trade for Mark Curtis on March 31, 1988.

Q   What is Ryne Sandberg's lifetime batting average?

A   .285

Q   What was the opening day lineup in 1980?

A   L. Randle, second base; I. DeJesus, shortstop; B. Buckner, first base; D. Kingman, leftfield; K. Henderson, rightfield; S. Ontiveros, third base; C. Lexcano, centerfield; T. Blackwell, catcher; R. Reuschel, pitcher.

Q   What was the opening day lineup in 1981?

A   I. DeJesus, shortstop; J. Strain, second base; B. Buckner, first base; S. Henderson, leftfield; L. Durham, rightfield; K. Reitz, third base; S. Thompson, centerfield' T. Blackwell, catcher; R. Reuschel, pitcher.

Q   What was the opening day lineup in 1982?
A   B. Willis, second base; L. Bowa, shortstop; B. Buckner, first base; L. Durham, rightfield; K. Moreland, catcher; S. Henderson, leftfield; R. Sandberg, third base; T. Waller, centerfield; D. Bird, pitcher.

Q   What was the opening day lineup in 1983?
A   M. Hall, leftfield; R. Sandberg, second base; B. Buckner, first base; L. Durham, centerfield; R. Cey, third base; K. Moreland, rightfield; J. Davis, catcher; L. Bowa, shortstop; F. Jenkins, pitcher.

Q   What was the opening day lineup in 1984?
A   B. Dernier, centerfield; R. Sandberg, second base; G. Matthews, leftfield; R. Cey, third base; K. Moreland, rightfield; J. Davis, catcher; L. Durham, first base; L. Bowa, shortstop; D. Ruthven, pitcher.

Q   Who had the most saves of any pitcher on the Cubs pitching staff in 1989?
A   Mitch Williams, with 36.

Q   Who pitched in the most innings on the Cubs pitching staff in 1989?
A   Greg Maddux, with 238 innings.

Q   Who had the most strikeouts of any of the Cub pitchers in 1989?
A   Rick Sutcliffe

Q   What pitcher won the most games for the Cubs in 1980?
A   Lynn McGlothen, with 12.

Q   Who won the most games for the Cubs in 1981?
A   Mike Krukow, with 9.

Q   Who won the most games for the Cubs in 1982?
A   Ferguson Jenkins, with 14.

Q   Who won the most games for the Cubs in 1983?
A   Chuck Rainey, with 14.

Q   Who won the most games for the Cubs in 1984?
A   Rick Sutcliffe, with 16.

Q   Who won the most games for the Cubs in 1985?
A   Dennis Eckersley, with 11.

Q   Who won the most games for the Cubs in 1986?
A   Lee Smith and Scott Sanderson each won 9.

Q   Who won the most games for the Cubs in 1987?
A   Rick Sutcliffe

Q   Who won the most games for the Cubs in 1988?
A   Greg Maddux, with 18.

Q   Who won the most games for the Cubs in 1989?
A   Greg Maddux, with 19.

Q   Who was the leading Cub reliever in 1980?
A   Rick Sutter, with 28 saves.

Q   Who was the leading Cub reliever in 1981?
A   Dick Tidrow, with nine saves.

Q   Who was the leading Cub reliever in 1982?
A   Lee Smith, with 17 saves.

Q   Who was the leading Cub reliever in 1983?
A   Lee Smith, with 29 saves.

Q   Who was the leading Cub reliever in 1984?
A   Lee Smith, with 33 saves.

Q   Who was the leading Cub reliever in 1985?
A   Lee Smith, with 33 saves.

Q Who was the leading Cub reliever in 1986?
A Lee Smith, with 31 saves.

Q Who was the leading Cub reliever in 1987?
A Lee Smith, with 36 saves.

Q Who was the leading Cub reliever in 1988?
A "Goose" Gossage, with 13 saves.

Q Who was the leading Cub reliever in 1989?
A Mitch Williams, with 36 saves.

Q What was Andre Dossin's batting average in 1989?
A .252

Q What was Shawon Dunston's batting average in 1989?
A .278

Q What was Lou Salazar's batting average in 1989?
A .282

Q What did Jerome Walton hit in 1989?
A .293

Q What was the opening day lineup in 1985?
A B. Dernier, centerfield; R. Sandberg, second base; G. Matthews, leftfield; L. Durham, first base; K. Moreland, rightfield; R. Cey, third base; J. Davis, catcher; S. Dunston, shortstop; R. Sutcliffe, pitcher.

Q What was the opening day lineup in 1986?
A B. Dernier, centerfield; M. Trillo, third base; R. Sandberg, second base; K. Moreland, rightfield; L. Durham, first base; J. Davis, catcher; B. Dayett, leftfield; S. Dunston, shortstop; R. Sutcliffe, pitcher.

Q   What was the opening day lineup in 1987?
A   B. Dernier, centerfield; R. Sandberg, second base; A. Dawson, rightfield; K. Moreland, third base; J. Davis, catcher; B. Dayett, leftfield; L. Durham, first base; S. Dunston, shortstop; R. Sutcliffe, pitcher.

Q   What was the opening day lineup in 1988?
A   D. Martinez, centerfield; R. Sandberg, second base; A. Dawson, rightfield; L. Durham, first base; R. Palmeiro, leftfield; J. Davis, catcher; V. Law, third base; S. Dunston, shortstop; R. Sutcliffe, pitcher.

Q   Who was the first Chicago Cub player to have his uniform retired?
A   Ernie Banks in August 1982

Q   When was Billy Williams' uniform retired?
A   August of 1987

Q   What was the largest attendance for a season by the Cubs?
A   1989 (2,491,942 at Wrigley Field)

Q   How long has Steve Stone been broadcasting with Harry Caray?
A   Stone retired from baseball in June 1982. It was his sixth consecutive year with WGN.

Q   What year did the Cubs win their first National League Eastern Division Championship?
A   1984

Q   What year was Dallas Green named Executive of the Year?
A   1984

Q   What pitcher on the Chicago Cubs had the most saves in 1989?
A   Mitch Williams, with 36.

Q   Jerome Walton had the longest hitting streak in 1989. How long was it?

A   Thirty games, the longest in Cub history.

Q   How many 300 hitters did the Cubs have in 1989?

A   Two, Dave Smith and Mark Grace.

Q   What member of the Cubs won the Silver Slugger Award in 1989?

A   Ryne Sandberg

Q   Who won the most games for the Cubs in 1989?

A   Greg Maddux won 19.

Q   Who had the lowest ERA of the Cub pitchers in 1989?

A   Les Lancaster, with 1.36.

Q   What pitcher appeared in the most games in 1989?

A   Mitch Williams, who appeared in 76.

Q   Who was the starting pitcher in the most games in 1989?

A   Greg Maddux, with 35.

Q   Who had the most complete games of the Cubs pitching staff in 1989?

A   Greg Maddux, with seven.

Q   Who pitched the most shutouts for the Cubs in 1989?

A   Mike Bielecki

Q   Who was the manager when the Cubs reached post-season play in 1984?

A   Jim Frey, who is now the Cubs general manager.

Q   Every post-season series has a hero and a goat. Who was the hero of the 1989 playoffs for San Francisco?

A   Will Clark. Clark had 13 hits in 20 times at bat (including three doubles, a triple, and two homers) and drove in eight runs. His batting average was .650.

Q   Who was the hero for the Chicago Cubs in the 1989 Championship Series?

A   Mark Grace. Mark got 11 hits in 17 times at bat (including three doubles, a triple, and a homerun), and he drove in eight runs. His batting average was .647.

Q   Who was the goat for the Chicago Cubs in the 1989 post-season series?

A   Andre Dawson, who got only two hits in 19 times at bat, for a batting average of .105.

Q   Who was the only Chicago Cub pitcher to be credited with a victory in the 1989 Championship Series?

A   Les Lancaster

Q   Who were the pitchers who were charged with the four losses?

A   Mike Bielecki, Greg Maddux, Les Lancaster, and Steve Wilson.

Q   What pitchers besides Maddux won over 10 games for the Cubs in 1989?

A   Mike Bielecki won 18 and lost 7; Rick Sutcliffe won 16 and lost 11; and Scott Sanderson won 11 and lost 9.

Q   What pitcher on the Chicago Cubs had the most saves in 1989?

A   Mitch Williams saved 36 games, was called the winner four times, and lost four times.

Q   Who led the Cubs in homeruns in 1989?

A   Ryne Sandberg, who had 30 homeruns.

Q   Who hit the second highest number of homeruns for the Cubs in 1989?

A   Andre Dawson had 21 homers.

Q   Who drove in the most runs for the Cubs in 1989?

A   Mark Grace drove in 79, Andre Dawson drove in 77, and Ryne Sandberg drove in 76.

Q   Who is the first Cub pitcher to win 18 or more games in one season since Ferguson Jenkins in 1972?

A   Greg Maddux. He won 19 games in 1989.

Q   How many players from the 1984 Cub team were on the 1989 team?

A   Three: Ryne Sandberg, Rick Sutcliffe, and Scott Sanderson.

Q   Who was the third base coach when the Cubs reached post-season play in 1984?

A   Don Zimmer

Q   Who had the highest batting average for the Cubs in 1984?

A   Ryne Sandberg hit .314. Gary Matthews was second with .291.

Q   Who was the leading pitcher for the Cubs in 1984?

A   Rick Sutcliffe, who came to the Cubs in mid-season, won 16 and lost 1.

Q   Who were the other ten or more game winners?

A   Steve "Rainbow" Trout won 13 and lost 7. Tim Stoddard won 10 and lost 6, and Dennis Eckersley won 10 and lost 8.

Q   Who led the Cubs in homeruns in 1984?

A   Ron Cey had 25 round trippers, besting Leon Durham, who had 23.

109

Q   Who drove in the most runs in 1984 for the Cubs?

A   Ron Cey had 97, beating Leon Durham by one. Jody Davis had 94; Ryne Sandberg had 84; Gary Matthews had 82; and Keith Moreland had 80.

Q   Who won the National League Championship in 1984?

A   San Diego defeated the Chicago Cubs three games to two.

Q   Who won the first game?

A   The Cubs won 13-0 behind the pitching of Rick Sutcliffe and Warren Brusstar.

Q   What other nicknames have the Chicago National League baseball teams had besides the White Stockings and the Cubs?

A   They were formerly known as the Colts and also as the Orphans.

Q   When was the first night game played at Wrigley Field?

A   August 8, 1988.

Q   When were the Chicago Cubs sold to the Tribune Company?

A   1981

Q   Did Joe Altobelli ever manage in the Majors?

A   Yes. He managed the San Francisco Giants from 1977 through 1979, and he managed Baltimore in 1983, 1984, and part of 1985.

Q   Who won the National League pennant in 1980?

A   The Philadelphia Phillies

Q   Who won the National League pennant in 1981?

A   The Los Angeles Dodgers

Q   Who won the National League pennant in 1982?

A   The St. Louis Cardinals

Q   Who won the National League pennant in 1983?
A   The Philadelphia Phillies

Q   Who won the National League pennant in 1984?
A   The San Diego Padres

Q   Who won the National League pennant in 1985?
A   The St. Louis Cardinals

Q   Who won the National League pennant in 1986?
A   The New York Mets

Q   Who won the National League pennant in 1987?
A   The St. Louis Cardinals

Q   Who won the National League pennant in 1988?
A   The Los Angeles Dodgers

Q   Who won the National League pennant in 1989?
A   The San Francisco Giants

Q   Who won the batting crown in the National League in 1980?
A   Bill Buckner hit .324.

Q   Who won the National League batting title in 1981
A   Bill Madlock hit .341.

Q   Who won the batting title in the National League in 1982?
A   Al Oliver, with .331.

Q   Who won the batting crown in the National League in 1983?
A   Bill Madlock, with .323.

Q   Who won the batting title in the National League in 1984?
A   Tony Gwynn, with .351.

Q   Who won the National League batting crown in 1985?
A   Willie McGee, with .353.

Q   Who won the batting championship in the National League in 1986?

A   Tim Raines hit .334.

Q   Who won the National League batting championship in 1987?

A   Tony Gwynn hit .370.

Q   Who won the National League batting title in 1988?

A   Tony Gwynn with .313.

Q   Who won the batting championship in the National League in 1989?

A   Tony Gwynn hit .336.

CHAPTER SIX
THE CHICAGO CUBS
AND THE WORLD SERIES

Q   When did the World Series, as we see it now, start?

A   In 1903, between Pittsburgh and Boston.

Q   Who won the Chicago all-Chicago World Series of 1906?

A   It was considered one of the greatest of all World Series upsets in the victory of the White Sox over the Cubs, four games to two.

Q   What was the first year the Chicago Cubs were in the World Series?

A   In 1906, playing against the Chicago White Sox. The White Sox won in six games.

Q   What was the second time the Cubs played in the World Series?

A   In 1907 the Chicago Cubs played the Detroit Tigers and won, winning four games to none and tying one.

Q   What was the second year the Chicago Cubs won the World Series?

A   In 1908 they defeated the Detroit Tigers in five games, four games to one, for their second victory in a row over the Tigers.

Q   Who was in the World Series of 1910?
A   The Philadelphia Athletics defeated the Chicago Cubs in five games.

Q   Did Babe Ruth ever pitch in the World Series?
A   Yes, in 1916 and 1918.

Q   How many games did Babe Ruth pitch in in the 1918 World Series?
A   Two

Q   Was Babe Ruth credited with a win in the 1918 World Series?
a   Yes, twice. He won two ballgames.

Q   Who won the Series of 1918?
A   The Boston Red Sox defeated the Cubs four games to two.

Q   Did Babe Ruth hit any homeruns in the 1918 World Series?
A   No

Q   What was Babe Ruth's batting average in the 1918 World Series?
A   Ruth went to bat five times and got one hit for a .200 average.

Q   Who were the winning pitchers for the World Series in 1918?
A   Carl Mays won two for Boston, as did Babe Ruth.

Q   Who were the Cubs' losing pitchers in the World Series in 1918?
A   "Hippo" Vaughn and "Lefty" Tyler and "Shufflin Phil" Douglas.

Q   The Cubs only won 2 games in their first World Series. Who were the winning pitchers?
A   "Three Finger" Brown and Ed Reulbach

114

Q   The Cubs won their first World Series in 1907. Who were their winning pitchers?

A   "Three Finger" Brown, Ed Reulbach, Jack Pfiester, and Orval Overall.

Q   Who was the Cubs' leading hitter in the World Series of 1907?

A   Hank Steinfeldt. He got eight hits at 17 times at bat for a .471 average.

Q   When did the Cubs win their second World Series?

A   In 1908 they defeated the Detroit Tigers in five games.

Q   Who were the winning pitchers for the Cubs in the 1908 World Series?

A   Orval Overall won two and so did "Three Finger" Brown.

Q   Who were the leading hitters for the Cubs in the 1908 World Series?

A   Frank Chance hit .421, "Wild Fire" Schulte hit .389, and Johnny Evers hit .350.

Q   When was the first time the Cubs met the Philadelphia Athletics in a World Series?

A   1910

Q   Who won the World Series of 1910?

A   Philadelphia won in five games.

Q   Who won the only game for the Cubs in the 1910 World Series?

A   "Three Finger" Brown won the Cubs' only victory and lost two times.

Q   Who were the leading hitters for the Cubs in the 1910 World Series?

A   Frank Chance hit .353, "Wild Fire" Schulte hit .353, and Joe Tinker hit .333.

Q   What pitcher won three games for the Philadelphia Athletics against the Cubs in the 1910 World Series?
A   Jack Coombs

Q   Who was the only pitcher in the World Series history to bat anyplace but ninth in the batting order?
A   In 1918 Babe Ruth batted sixth in the lineup, got one triple, sacrificed once, and grounded out.

Q   How many times did Chicago win the National League pennant before 1900?
A   Six times in the Old National League — 1876, 1880, 1881, 1882, 1885, and 1886.

Q   Who was in the World Series in 1929?
A   The Philadelphia Athletics defeated the Chicago Cubs in five games.

Q   Who was the surprise winning pitcher for Philadelphia in the first game in the 1929 World Series?
A   Howard Ehmke, who had pitched in only 55 innings during the regular season.

Q   How many men did Ehmke strike out in the first game of the World Series in 1929?
A   Thirteen — which was a Series record at that time.

Q   Who won the second game of the Series in 1929?
A   Philadelphia

Q   Who was the winning pitcher of the second game of the World Series in 1929?
A   George Earnshaw

Q   What is the smallest crowd to ever see a World Series game?
A   6,210; between the Detroit Tigers and the Chicago Cubs on October 14, 1908. The Cubs won the game 2–0. It was the fifth game of the Series.

116

Q What was the smallest attendance for a five-game World Series?
A 62,232 people watched the Chicago Cubs and the Detroit Tigers in 1908.

Q What was the smallest attendance for a six-game series?
A 99,845 saw the Chicago White Sox defeat the Chicago Cubs in 1906.

Q What was the smallest winning player share in a World Series?
A $1,102.51 went to the Boston Red Sox in the World Series when they played the Chicago Cubs in 1918.

Q What was the smallest losing players in a World Series?
A $439.50 is what the Chicago Cubs received in the World Series against the Chicago White Sox in 1906.

Q What was the shortest game by minutes in a World Series?
A It took one hour and 25 minutes for the Chicago Cubs to defeat the Detroit Tigers 2–0 in Detroit on October 14, 1908.

Q Four regulars hit over .300 in the 1929 World Series for the Cubs. Who were they?
A Hack Wilson hit .471, Charlie Grimm hit .389, Riggs Stephenson hit .316, and Kiki Cuyler hit an even .300.

Q Who were the pitchers on the staff of the Chicago Cubs that played in the 1929 World Series?
A Guy Bush, Pat Malone, Charlie Root, Hal Carlson, "Sheriff" Blake, and Art Nehf.

Q Who was the first baseman for the Chicago Cubs in the 1929 World Series?
A Charlie Grimm

Q   Who was the second baseman for the Chicago Cubs in the 1929 World Series?

A   Rogers Hornsby

Q   Who was the shortstop for the Chicago Cubs in the 1929 World Series?

A   "Woody" English

Q   Who was the third baseman for the Chicago Cubs in the 1929 World Series?

A   Norm MacMillan

Q   How many Cubs hit homeruns in the 1929 World Series?

A   One, Charlie Grimm.

Q   How many Philadelphia Athletics hit homeruns in the 1929 World Series?

A   There were six homeruns: two by Jimmy Foxx, two by Mule Haas, and two by Al Simmons.

Q   How many games did Lefty Grove win in the 1929 World Series?

A   None

Q   Who was the winning pitcher for the Cubs in their only victory in the 1929 World Series?

A   Guy Bush

Q   Who were the losing pitchers for the Cubs in the 1929 World Series?

A   Pat Malone lost twice, Charlie Root lost once, and "Sheriff" Blake lost once.

Q   Who was the goat in the World Series in 1929?

A   Hack Wilson, who lost a fly ball in the sun, which went for a homerun.

Q   What was the most outstanding thing of the 1929 World Series?

A   In the fourth game the cubs were ahead 8–0 when Philadelphia came to bat in the seventh inning and scored 10 times.

Q   Who were the leading hitters for the Philadelphia Athletics in the 1929 World Series?

A   Jimmy Dykes had a .421 average, and Mike Cochrane had a .400 average.

Q   What was the Cubs biggest disappointment at the plate during the 1929 World Series?

A   Rogers Hornsby, the Most Valuable Player of the league, hit only .238 and struck out eight times.

Q   Who was the manager of the Cubs in the 1929 World Series?

A   Joe McCarthy

Q   Who was the manager of the Cubs in the 1918 World Series?

A   Fred Mitchell

Q   Who was the pitcher who had the lead of 8–0 going into the seventh inning when Philadelphia scored 10 times?

A   Charlie Root

Q   Who was the losing pitcher for the Cubs the day they had the 8–0 lead and lost 10–8 in the 1929 World Series?

A   "Sheriff" Blake

Q   What was the regular infield for the Cubs in the 1932 World Series?

A   Charlie Grimm was at first, Billy Herman at second, "Woody" English played third, and Billy Jurges was shortstop.

Q   What was the outfield for the Cubs in the 1932 World Series?

A   Riggs Stephenson, Frank Demaree, and Kiki Cuyler.

Q   Who was the catcher for the Cubs in the 1932 World Series?
A   Gabby Hartnett

Q   Who were the main pitchers for the Cubs in the 1932 World Series?
A   Pat Malone, Lon Warneke, Charlie Root, Jake May, Guy Bush, and Burly Grimes.

Q   What was the Yankee infield for the 1932 World Series?
A   Lou Gehrig at first, Tony Lazzeri at second, Joe Sewell at third, and Frank Crosetti at shortstop.

Q   Who was in the outfield for the Yankees in the 1932 World Series?
A   Babe Ruth, Ben Chapman, and Earl Coombs.

Q   Who was the catcher for the Yankees in the 1932 World Series?
A   Bill Dickey

Q   When Babe Ruth pointed to the stands to indicate he was going to hit a homerun in the 1932 World Series, where was the game played?
A   Chicago's Wrigley Field

Q   When Babe Ruth pointed to the stands to indicate he was going to hit a homerun for the next pitch, who was pitching for Chicago?
A   Charlie Root

Q   Who won the game in which Babe Ruth pointed to the stands to indicate he was going to hit a homerun in the 1932 World Series?
A   New York, 7–5.

Q What inning was it in which Babe Ruth pointed to the stands to indicate he was going to hit a homerun in the 1932 World Series?

A The fifth inning. It was the third game.

Q How many games in a row did the Chicago Cubs win in September to enable them to win the pennant in 1935?

A 21 consecutive games

Q The Cubs won the first game of the 1935 World Series with what pitcher throwing a shutout against the Detroit Tigers?

A Lon Warneke

Q Who won the second game of the 1935 World Series?

A The Detroit Tigers won 8–3.

Q The third game of the World Series went into extra innings. How many innings did it go and who won the game?

A The Tigers defeated the Cubs 6–5 in 11 innings.

Q Who won the fourth game of the World Series of 1935?

A The Detroit Tigers defeated Chicago behind the pitching of General Crowder.

Q Who won the fifth game of the World Series in 1935?

A Lon Warneke defeated the Tigers for the second time. This time the Tigers got seven hits.

Q Who won the sixth game of the World Series in 1935?

A The Detroit Tigers won 4–3.

Q Who pitched for the Tigers in the sixth and final game of the World Series in 1935?

A Tommy Bridges

Q Who pitched for the Chicago Cubs in the sixth and final game of the World Series in 1935?

A Larry French

Q   Who played third base for the Cubs in the 1935 World Series?
A   Stan Hack

Q   Who was the shortstop for the Cubs in the 1935 World Series?
A   Billy Jurges

Q   Who played in the outfield for the Cubs in the 1935 World Series?
A   Augie Galan, Fred Lindstrom, Frank Demaree, and Chuck Klein patrolled the outfield.

Q   Who was the catcher for the Cubs in the 1935 World Series?
A   Gabby Hartnett

Q   Who won the National League pennant in 1932?
A   The Chicago Cubs

Q   Who did the Cubs play in the 1932 World Series?
A   The New York Yankees

Q   Who managed the Yankees in the 1932 World Series?
A   Joe McCarthy, who had formerly managed the Chicago Cubs.

Q   Did Joe McCarthy ever play in the Major Leagues?
A   No

Q   How many games did the Cubs win in the 1932 World Series?
A   None

Q   Who were the leading pitchers for the New York Yankees in the 1932 World Series?
A   Cy Moore, Lefty Gomez, Red Ruffing, and George Pitgrass.

Q   Who were the losing pitchers for the Cubs in the 1932 World Series?

A   Lon Warneke, Charlie Root, Guy Bush, and Frank May.

Q   Who played third base for the Tigers in the 1935 World Series?

A   Marv Owen played third the first two games, and "Flea" Clifton played the last four.

Q   Did any Tigers hit a homerun in the 1935 World Series?

A   Hank Greenberg, in the second game.

Q   In the sixth game of the 1935 World Series and the score tied, who opened the ninth inning with a triple?

A   Stan Hack

Q   Who led the Tigers in batting in the World Series in 1935?

A   Pete Fox

Q   Who was the second best hitter for the Tigers in the 1935 World Series?

A   Charlie Gehringer, with .375.

Q   Who was the best hitter for the Cubs in the 1935 World Series?

A   Billy Herman, with .333.

Q   The Cubs have been in ten World Series. How many have they won?

A   They won two and lost eight.

Q,   Did the Cubs ever play a tie game in a World Series?

A   Yes, in 1907 one game was called on account of darkness.

Q   Frank Secory umpired for 18 years in the National League. did he ever play in a World Series?

A   Yes. Frank was in five games in the 1945 w as the pinch-hitter. He got two hits at five times at bat.

Q   Who played first base for the Cubs in the 1935 World Series?
A   Phil Cavarretta

Q   Who played second base for the Cubs in the 1935 World Series?
A   Billy Herman

Q   Who played third base for the Cubs in the 1935 World Series?
A   Stan Hack

Q   Who was the shortstop for the Cubs in the 1935 World Series?
A   Billy Jurges

Q   Who played in the outfield for the Cubs in the 1935 World Series?
A   Augie Galan, Fred Lindstrom, Frank Demaree, and Chuck Klein patrolled the outfield in the Series of 1935.

Q   Who was the catcher for the Cubs in the 1935 World Series?
A   Gabby Hartnett

Q   Who won the National League pennant in 1932?
A   The Chicago Cubs

Q   Who did the Cubs play in the World Series of 1932?
A   The New York Yankees

Q   Who managed the Yankees in the 1932 World Series?
A   Joe McCarthy, who had formerly managed the Chicago Cubs.

Q   Did Joe McCarthy ever play in the major leagues?
A   No

Q   How many games did the Cubs win in the 1932 World Series?
A   None

Q Who was the batting hero of the sixth game of the World Series in 1935?

A Goose Goslin got a single in the ninth inning, driving in Mickey Cochrane to break a 3-3 tie and give Detroit the World Championship.

Q Who hit homeruns for the Cubs in the 1935 World Series?

A Frank Demaree hit two homers; Billy Herman hit one; Chuck Klein hit one; and Gabby Hartnett hit one.

Q Who were the losing pitchers in the four games that the Cubs lost in the 1935 World Series?

A Larry French lost twice, Charlie Root lost once, and Carleton also lost one.

Q Who were the winning pitchers for the Tigers in the 1935 World Series?

A General Crowder won one; Schoolboy Rowe won one; and Tommy Bridges won two.

Q Who was the leading batter for the Cubs in the 1935 World Series?

A Billy Herman hit .333, as did Chuck Klein.

Q Who played first base for the Cubs in the 1935 World Series?

A Phil Cavarratta

Q Who played second base for the Cubs in the 1935 World Series?

A Billy Herman

Q Who were the winning pitchers for the Yankees in the four game series with the Cubs in 1938?

A Red Ruffing won two games, Monte Pearson and "Lefty" Gomez each won one game.

Q How many Cubs hit homeruns in the 1938 World Series?

A Two: Joe Marty and Ken O'Dea.

Q   How many Yankees hit homeruns in the 1938 World Series?

A   Five: Bill Dickey, Joe Gordon, Joe DiMaggio, Frank Crosetti, and Tommy Henrich.

Q   Who was the first baseman for the Detroit Tigers in the 1935 World Series?

A   Hank Greenberg played first in the first two games.

Q   Why didn't Hank Greenberg play more than the first two games in the 1935 World Series?

A   He broke his wrist in the second game.

Q   Who placed first base for the Tigers in the 1935 World Series in third, fourth, fifth, and sixth games?

A   Marv Owen

Q   Who were the outfielders for the Tigers in the 1935 World Series?

A   Jo-Jo White, Goose Goslin, and Pete Fox.

Q   Who was the second baseman for the Tigers in the 1935 World Series?

A   Charlie Gehringer

Q   Who was the shortstop for the Tigers in the 1935 World Series?

A   Billy Rogell

Q   Who was the catcher for the Cubs in the 1938 World Series?

A   Gabby Hartnett

Q   Who was the first baseman for the Cubs in the World Series in 1938?

A   "Rip" Collins

Q   Who was the shortstop for the Cubs in the World Series in 1938?

A   Billy Jurges

Q   Who shared the outfield duties in the World Series of 1938 with Carl Reynolds, Frank Demaree and Phil Cavarretta?

A   Joe Marty.

Q   Who was the leading hitter for the Cubs in the World Series in 1938?

A   Joe Marty hit an even .500.

Q   Who hit homeruns for the Cubs in the World Series of 1938?

A   Ken O'Dea and Joe Marty

Q   Dizzy Dean pitched one game for the Cubs in the World Series of 1938. He went to bat three times. How many hits did he get?

A   Two

Q   Who were the losing pitchers in the World Series of 1938?

A   Bill Lee lost two games, Dizzy Dean lost one, and Clay Bryant lost one.

Q   Who was the manager of the Yankees in the World Series of 1938?

A   Joe McCarthy, who had formerly managed the Cubs.

Q   How many games did the World Series of 1938 go?

A   Four games

Q   Who played third base for the Cubs in the World Series of 1938?

A   Stan Hack

Q   Who played second base for the Cubs in the World Series of 1938?

A   Billy Herman

Q   Who played left field for the Cubs in the World Series of 1938?

A   Frank Demaree

Q   Who played right field for the Cubs in the World Series of 1938?
A   Phil Cavarratta

Q   Who was the centerfielder for the Cubs in the World Series of 1938?
A   Carl Reynolds and Joe Marty

Q   Who was the catcher for the Cubs in the World Series of 1938?
A   Gabby Hartnett

Q   Who was the first baseman for the Cubs in the World Series of 1938?
A   "Rip" Collins

Q   Who was the shortstop for the Cubs in the World Series of 1938?
A   Billy Jurges

Q   Who was the first baseman for the Yankees in the 1938 World Series?
A   Lou Gehrig

Q   Who was the second baseman for the Yankees in the 1938 World Series?
A   Joe Gordon

Q   Who was the third baseman for the Yankees in the 1938 World Series?
A   Red Rolfe

Q   Who was the shortstop for the Yankees in the 1938 World Series?
A   Frank Cosetti

Q Who played leftfield for the Yankees in the 1938 World Series?

A George Selkirk and Myron Hoag

Q Who played centerfield for the Yankees in the 1938 World Series?

A Joe DiMaggio

Q Who played rightfield for the Yankees in the 1938 World Series?

A Tom Henrich

Q Who was the catcher for the Yankees in the 1938 World Series?

A Bill Dickey

Q What was the last year the Cubs were in the World Series?
A 1945

Q Who were the Cubs' opponents in the World Series in 1945?
A The Detroit Tigers

Q How many games did the World Series go in 1945?
A Seven

Q Who won the first game of the World Series in 1945?
A The Cubs, behind the pitching of Hank Borowy.

Q Who won the second game of the World Series in 1945?
A The Tigers won 4-1.

Q Who won the third game of the World Series in 1945?
A Chicago, 3-1.

Q How many hits did the Tigers get in the third game of the World Series in 1945?
A One

Q   Who got the only hit that the Tigers got in the third game of the World Series in 1945?

A   Rudy York

Q   What inning did Rudy York get the only hit in the third gameof the World Series in 1945?

A   Second inning

Q   Who pitched the one-hit game for the Cubs in the third game of the World Series in 1945?

A   Claude Passeau

Q   Who won the fourth game of the World Series in 1945?

A   Detroit

Q   Who won the fifth game of the World Series in 1945?

A   Detroit

Q   Who won the sixth game of the World Series in 1945?

A   Chicago

Q   How many innings did the sixth game of the World Series of 1945 go?

A   Twelve innings

Q   Who drove in the winning run in the sixth game of the World Series of 1945?

A   Stan Hack

Q   Who won the seventh and final game of the World Series of 1945?

A   The Detroit Tigers

Q   Who drove in the winning run in the seventh and final game of the World Series of 1945?

A   Paul Richards

Q   Who was the Cubs' second baseman in the World Series of 1945?

A   Don Johnson

Q   Who was the Cubs' third baseman in the World Series of 1945?

A   Stan Hack

Q   Who was the Cubs' first baseman in the World Series of 1945?

A   Phil Cavarratta

Q   Who was the Cubs' shortstop in the World Series of 1945?
A   Roy Hughes

Q   Who played in the outfield for the Cubs in the World Series of 1945?

A   "Peanuts" Lowrey, Andy Pafko, and Billy Nicholson.

Q   Who caught for the Cubs in the World Series of 1945?

A   Mickey Livingston caught six games, Paul Gillespie and Dewey Williams caught parts of another.

Q   Who was the Cubs' leading batter in the World Series of 1945?

A   Phil Cavarratta, with .423.

Q   How many homeruns did the Cubs hit in the World Series of 1945?

A   One, by Phil Cavarratta.

Q   The Cubs won three games in the World Series of 1945. Who were the winning pitchers?

A   Hank Borowy won two games, and Claude Passeau won the other.

Q   Who was the batting hero for the Detroit Tigers in the World Series of 1945?

A   "Doc" Kramer hit .379 and Hank Greenberg hit .304 with two homeruns.

Q   In the World Series of 1945 when Claude Passeau pitched his masterpiece allowing only one hit, how many men did he walk?

A   One, Bob Swift.

Q   Who played in the World Series of 1938?

A   The Yankees and the Cubs

Q   Who won the World Series of 1938?

A   The New York Yankees

PART TWO

CHAPTER SEVEN
THE CHICAGO CUBS:
THE MANY BOYS OF SUMMER

Grover Cleveland Alexander, who was nicknamed "Pete," held a record of 90 shutouts during his career. He pitched four one-hitters in 1915 and 16 shutouts, which is still a major league high. In the 1926 World Series he won two games and came in and saved the last game, striking out Tony Lazzeri with the bases loaded. He pitched 20 years in the National League for the Phillies, Cubs, and Cardinals. He won 373 games and lost 208. Three times he won more than 30 games and six other times he won more than 20. He died in St. Paul, Minnesota, in 1950. He was admitted to baseball's Hall of Fame in 1938.

Cap Anson was the greatest player of the 19th century. He was a slugging first baseman and also manager of Chicago in the old National League. He played for 22 years and hit over .300 all but two of those years. Three times he led the league and he was the first batter to get 3,000 hits. His lifetime batting average was .334 and he hit .303 at the age of 45. Cap also led his National League club to 15 first division finishes, winning five pennants in 19 years. He died in Chicago in 1922. He was inducted into baseball's Hall of Fame in 1939.

Richie Ashburn spent 15 years in the big leagues: twelve with the Philadelphia Phillies, two with the Cubs, and one with the New York Mets. He had a lifetime batting average of .308. He stole 234 bases during his career. Not a long ball hitter, he had only 29 homeruns during his 15 years but was an excellent defensive outfielder. He came to the Cubs in January 1960 in a trade for John Buzhardt, Jim Woods, and Alvin Dark. The Cubs sold him to the New York Mets after the 1961 season for cash. Richie twice led the National League in batting in 1955 and again in 1958.

Ernie Banks played 19 years for the Chicago Cubs and delighted the Wrigley Field fans with his long and frequent homeruns. He was also known for his steady fielding and cheerful disposition. He hit 512 homeruns and five times hit over 40 in a single year. He had five grand slams in 1955 and in 1958 he hit 47 homers, which is the most ever hit by a shortstop. He was twice selected the Most Valuable Player in the National League, in 1958 and 1959. He led the League in homers three times and was inducted into the Hall of Fame in 1977. He played shortstop from 1953 until 1962 and at first base until he retired after the 1971 season.

Glenn Beckert joined the Cubs in 1965 and stayed with them through 1973. He was a second baseman. He went to San Diego in November of 1973 with Bobby Fenwick, in exchange for Jerry Morales. Glenn had a .283 lifetime batting average for his 11 years in the majors.

Mike Bielecki is a right-handed pitcher who was born in Baltimore, Maryland. He started out his minor league career in 1979, came up to Pittsburgh in 1984, went back to the minors, came back to Pittsburgh in 1985 and 1986, went to Vancouver in the Pacific Coast league n 1987, and came back to Pittsburgh at the end of the season. He was with Iowa in the American Association in 1988 and also with the Cubs. He came to the Cubs in a trade for Mike Curtis on March 31, 1988. Mike won 18 and lost seven as the Cubs won their divisional championship in 1989, giving him 30 victories against 26 defeats in his six years in the Major Leagues. In the

136

playoffs, Mike pitched in two games and was charged with one defeat. He had an earned run average of 3.65.

Bobby Bonds came from Riverside, California. He was a right-handed batter and also threw right-handed. He played for 14 years in the major leagues, starting out with San Francisco in 1968. He went to the Yankees in 1975, to the Angels in 1976, to the White Sox in 1978, and then went to Texas. In 1979 he was with Cleveland, in 1980 with the Cardinals, and in 1981 he had a brief appearance with the Cubs. He is the father of Barry Bonds, who is with Pittsburgh. Bobby had a lifetime batting average of .268 for his 14 years in the big leagues and had 332 homeruns.

Bill Bonham was a right-handed pitcher who played with the Cubs from 1971 through 1977. He went to Cincinnati in a trade for Woody Fryman and Bill Caudill. Bill was a native of Glendale, California. He won 75 games and lost 83 in his 10-year career in the National Leagues.

Hank Borowy came to the Cubs in July of 1945 from the Yankees for a reported sum of $97,000.00. Hank had pitched for the Yankees from 1942 until the sale. He had won 10 games for the Yankees in 1945 and then won 11 for the Cubs, making him a 21-game winner in both leagues. He stayed with the Cubs until the 1949 season, when he went to Philadelphia in a trade along with Eddie Waitkus, in exchange for Dutch Leonard and Monk Dubiel. He later went to Pittsburgh and then to Detroit. He finished his career with the Tigers in 1951. In his 10 years he won 108 and lost 82. In three World Series he won three and lost two, including two wins and two losses in the 1945 World Series with the Cubs. He is best remembered, though, for winning 10 games with the Yankees in 1945 and 11 with the Cubs in the same season.

Lou Boudreau was a great shortstop and hitter for the Cleveland Indians and took over the managing of the Indians at the tender age of 24. Six years later he hit .355 with 106 runs batted in as the Indians won the American League pennant and went on to win the

World Championship. The Indians were tied with the Boston Red Sox on the final day of the season and had to play a one-game playoff. Lou got four hits in four times at bat, including a homerun. He also was the one who devised the "Ted Williams shift." He later managed the Boston Red Sox, the Kansas City A's, and the Chicago Cubs, and was a broadcaster for the Chicago Cubs. He led the American League in batting in 1944 with a .327 average. His lifetime average for 15 years was .295 and he hit .273 in the World Series of 1948. He was elected to baseball's Hall of Fame in 1970.

Roger Bresnahan was called "The Duke of Tralee." He came from Toledo, Ohio, and died there in 1944. He played 17 years in the major leagues, starting out with Washington in 1897, going to Chicago in the National League in 1900, to Baltimore in 1901 and 1902, and to the Giants in 1902. He stayed there until 1909 when he went with the Cardinals and played there through 1912. He finished his career in 1915 with a three-year stint with the Chicago Cubs. In his 17 years he had a .279 batting average. He played in World Series of 1905, got five hits at 16 times at bat for a .313 batting average. He was famous as the battery mate of the great Christy Mathewson. Roger managed the St. Louis Cardinals in 1909, 1910, 1911, and 1912, and the Chicago Cubs in 1915.

Lou Brock came from Eldorado, Arkansas, the same town that produced "Schoolboy" Rowe of great fame in the 1930's and 1940's. Lou joined the Cubs in 1961. In 1964 the Cubs made one of the worst trades in the history of baseball. They sent Lou, Jack Spring, and Paul Toth in exchange for Ernie Broglio, Bobby Shantz, and Doug Clemens. Brock became a superstar, put in 15 years with the Cardinals, and wound up with a lifetime batting average of .293. He stole 938 bases during his career, (118 in 1974 alone). He played in three World Series and was a star in each. He got 34 hits in 87 times at bat for a .391 batting average. He had a total of 14 stolen bases, seven in 1967 and seven in 1968. He hit four homeruns. He led the National League in stolen bases on eight occasions and entered baseball's Hall of Fame in 1985.

Mordecai "Three Finger" Brown was the number-one pitcher, along with Chris Mathewson, in the early 1900's. He was a member of the Cubs' championship team of 1906, 1907, 1908, and 1910, and posted six consecutive 20-victory seasons. He got his nickname because as a youth he lost parts of two fingers in a feed cutter. But he overcame this handicap and used it to his advantage in developing one of the greatest curve balls ever. He won 239 games and lost 129 games in 14 years. In the four World Series he was in, he won five and lost four games. He died in February 1948 in Terre Haute, Indiana, and was admitted to baseball's Hall of Fame in 1949.

Clay Bryant was a right-handed pitcher from Madison Heights, Virginia. He pitched for the Chicago Cubs for six years, winning 32 and losing 20. In 1938 he won 19 and lost 11. He was in the 1938 World Series and was the loser in one game. The year before, he won nine and lost three. During the other four years that he pitched, he won only a total of four games.

Bill Buckner hails from Vallejo, California. He is a left-handed batter, throws left-handed, and plays mainly first base. He started his baseball career in 1968 with Ogden in the Pioneer League. He was with Albuquerque in 1969 and Spokane in the Pacific Coast League. He came to the Dodgers at the end of the 1969 season and started off the 1970 season with them. Buckner went back to Spokane and then returned to the Dodgers in 1971, where he stayed until 1976 when he was traded to the Chicago Cubs with infielder Ivan DeJesus and Jeff Albert for Rick Monday and Mike Garman. He remained with the Cubs until the middle of the 1984 season when he was traded to the Boston Red Sox for Dennis Eckersley and Mike Brumley. With Boston through the middle of the 1987 season, he went to California in the 1988 season and wound up with Kansas City, where he played in 1989. He has a 21-year career in the major leagues and a lifetime batting average of .290. He played in the 1974 World Series with Los Angeles and hit .250, getting five hits in 20 times at bat. In 1986 he played with the Red Sox and got six hits at 32 times at bat for a .188. In the 1986 World Series Bill let a routine bouncer hit by Mookie Wilson go through his legs; Ray

Knight then crossed the plate with a run that defeated the Red Sox in the sixth game.

Bob Buhl was in the big leagues for 15 years. He was with Milwaukee from 1953 to 1962 when he came to the Cubs in mid-season in a trade for Jack Curtis. Bob won 166 games and lost 132. He was with the Cubs for part of 1962 and all of 1963, 1964, and 1965, and part of 1966. Twice he was an 18-game winner when he was with Milwaukee. Bob is well remembered as one of the worst hitters of all time. In his 15 years in the big leagues, his batting average was .089, and in 1962 he went to bat 70 times and did not get a single base hit.

Smoky Burgess was a left-handed batter who played 18 years in the big leagues. He was a catcher, but he was known mainly for his pinch-hitting. In his 18-year career in the big leagues, he pinch-hit 507 times and was successful 145 times, for a batting average of .285. He started off with the Chicago Cubs in 1949, went to the Phillies in 1952, to the Reds in 1955, to Pittsburgh in 1959, and to the White Sox in 1964. He had a lifetime batting average of .295, ten points better than his average as a pinch-hitter.

Guy Bush was called "the Mississippi Mudcat." He came from Aberdeen, Mississippi, and he pitched for the Cubs from 1923 to 1935 when he went to Pittsburgh. He later went to the Boston Braves, the St. Louis Cardinals, and the Cincinnati Reds. In 17 years in the big leagues, he won 176 games and lost 136. He played in two World Series with the Cubs, winning one game and losing one. He is well remembered as the pitcher who gave up Babe Ruth's last homerun in 1935 when he was pitching for Pittsburgh. Guy died in Shannon, Mississippi, in July 1985.

Nixey Callahan came from Fitchburg, Massachusetts. He played with the Philadelphia Phillies in the old National League and then played with Chicago. He won 20 games in 1898 and in 1899 he won 21. Nixey went with the White Sox in 1901 and stayed there for three years. His eight-year career as a pitcher showed 99 wins and

140

73 losses. He died in Boston, Massachusetts, in October 1934. Nixey managed Chicago in the American League in 1903 and 1904 and again in 1912, 1913, and 1914. He managed Pittsburgh in 1916 and 1917 and also played in the outfield and in the infield. He had a batting average of .273 for his 13 years.

Harry Caray concluded his eighth year with the Cubs as a broadcaster in 1989. He was named the winner of the Ford C. Frick Award in January 1989 and was admitted to the Hall of Fame in July 1989. He was elected to the National Sportscasters and Sportswriters Hall of Fame in 1988. Before joining the Cubs' broadcasting team in 1982, Harry was the voice of the White Sox for 11 years (1971 through 1981). He had previously spent 25 years broadcasting the Cardinal games. In one season (1970) he announced the Oakland Athletic games.

Jose Cardenal came from Matanzas, Cuba. He spent 18 years in the big leagues and had a lifetime batting average of 275. He was with the Cubs from 1972 to 1978. An outfielder and a right-handed hitter who also threw right-handed, Jose was in one World Series with Kansas City in 1980 and got two hits in 10 times at bat for a .200 average.

Phil Cavarretta came out of Lane Tech High School in Chicago at the tender age of 18. He played with the Cubs in seven games at that age. In 1935 he became the regular first baseman and stayed with the Cubs through 1953. He managed the club in 1951 and 1952, went to the White Sox in 1954, and finished his 22-year career there in 1955. Phil had a .293 lifetime batting average, he was in three World Series with the Cubs, and had an average of .317 in those three years.

Ron Cey was called "the Penguin." He played for 17 years in the major leagues, mainly with the Los Angeles Dodgers (1971 through 1982). He came to the Cubs in 1983 and played with them for four years, before going to Oakland, where he finished his career in 1987 with the Oakland A's. His 17-year batting average was .261. He hit

316 homeruns during his career, and he played with the Dodgers in four World Series with a batting average of .253.

Frank Chance was nicknamed "The Peerless Leader." He was the first baseman in the Tinkers-to-Evers-to-Chance Chicago Cub infield. One of the finer hitters and fielders in the early 90's, he was recognized specially as the club's playing manager and gained his nickname when the Cubs won four pennants in five years, 1906–1910. The club's 116 victories in 1906 have been unmatched in major league history. Frank's lifetime batting average for 17 years was .297, and he hit .310 in four World Series. He died in Los Angeles in September of 1924 and entered baseball's Hall of Fame in 1946.

"Kiki" Cuyler was one of the National League's outstanding outfielders of his day. He was a good fielder and an excellent hitter and base runner. He hit over .310 in 10 of his 15 full seasons, hitting over .350 four times, and had a lifetime batting average of .321. Four times he led the league in stolen bases. He played for four pennant winners and his seventh game, eighth inning, bases loaded double off Walter Johnson won the 1925 World Series for the Pirates. He died in February of 1950 in Ann Arbor, Michigan, and entered baseball's Hall of Fame in 1968.

Jody Davis is a right-handed hitting catcher who came from Gainesville, Georgia. He joined the Cubs in 1981 and was their regular catcher until 1988 when he went to Atlanta near the end of the season. He played with Atlanta in 1989, and his nine-year batting average is .246.

Andre Dawson spent two years in the minor leagues before coming to Montreal in the latter part of 1976. He came to the Cubs as a free agent in January 1987 and played with them in 1987, 1988, and 1989. Andre was selected Rookie of the Year in the National League in 1977. His 13-year career batting average is .280 and he has 319 homeruns. In the championship playoffs in 1989, Andre went to bat 19 times and got only two hits for a .105 batting average. He is a native of Miami, Florida, and bats and throws right-handed.

"Dizzy" Dean was a legend in his own time. He came into the major leagues in 1930 and averaged over 24 wins for the first five full seasons. He won 30 and lost seven in 1934 when he pitched (along with his brother, Paul) the Cardinals to the World Championship. He won two games and lost one in the World Series with the Tigers. A broken toe, suffered in the 1937 All-Star Game, led to an injury that shortened his career. Dean came out of Lucas, Arkansas. He went to the Chicago Cubs in 1938 but his career was really ended by the line drive. He won 150 games and lost 83 in 12 years. "Dizzy" died in July of 1974 and was named to the Hall of Fame in 1953.

Frank Demaree was a right-handed batter who also threw right-handed. He came from Winters, California, and played for the Cubs from 1932 to 1939 when he went to the Giants, then the Braves, the Cardinals, and the Browns. Frank was a centerfielder. In his 12-year career he had a lifetime batting average of .299. He was with the Cubs in three World Series: 1932, 1935, and 1938; and with the Cardinals in 1943. He had a batting average of .214 in his four World Series.

Bob Dernier came from Kansas City and joined the Philadelphia Philies in 1980. He came to the Cubs in 1984 and spent four seasons with Chicago before joining the Phillies in 1988. He played there in 1988 and 1989. The lifetime batting average for this right-handed hitting outfielder for his 10 years in the National League is .255.

Paul Derringer was called the "Springfield Rifle." He came from Springfield, Kentucky, and pitched in the major leagues for 15 years, winning 223 games and losing 212. He was in four World Series: with the Cardinals in 1931, the Reds in 1939 and 1940, and the Cubs in 1945. He won two games and lost four. He spent three years with the Cubs: 1943, 1944, and 1945. Paul was a 20-game winner on four occasions when he pitched for the Reds, winning 25 in 1939 and losing only seven for his best record when he led the League with the highest percentage, .781.

Moe Drabowsky came from Ozanna, Poland. He joined the Cubs in 1956, stayed with them until 1960, and then went to Milwaukee, Cincinnati, Kansas City, Baltimore, the Cardinals, and the White Sox. In his 17 years in the big leagues, Moe won 88 games and lost 105. He was a right-handed pitcher. He was in the World Series in 1966 and 1970 with Baltimore and was credited with one win.

Hugh Duffy was an outfielder with Chicago, Boston, Milwaukee and Philadelphia for 17 years in the National League. He started his career in 1888 and finished up in 1906. He was one of the hardest hitters in the game, although he was only 5'7". He hit .300 ten straight times and hit .438 in 1894, the highest average of all time. He closed out his 17-year career as a player/manager of the Phillies in 1906 and died in Boston in October 1954. Hugh entered baseball's Hall of Fame in 1945.

Shawon Dunston is a right-handed hitting shortstop. He came up to the Cubs in 1985 and has a five-year batting average of .255. He became the regular shortstop in 1986. In the playoffs of 1989 Dunston got six hits in 19 times at bat for a .316 batting average. He hails from Brooklyn, New York, and has the unusual nickname of "Thunderpup."

Leon Durham was known as "The Bull." He started his major league career with the Cardinals in 1980 and came to the Cubs in 1981, where he remained until 1988 when he went to Cincinnati. He was released by Cincinnati in 1989. His nine-year record showed a batting average of .278. Leon, who came from Cincinnati, Ohio, was an outfielder and first baseman.

Leo Durocher started his 17-year career as a player with the New York Yankees in 1925. He later went to Cincinnati, the St. Louis Cardinals, and the Brooklyn Dodgers. He played in two World

Series and had a lifetime batting average of .247. He was a short-stop, but Leo is mainly remembered for his managing. He managed Brooklyn from 1939 until 1948. In the middle of 1948 he went to the New York Giants. He managed the Cubs from 1966 until the middle of 1972 and managed Houston for the balance of 1972 and 1973.

Dennis Eckersley, after three years in the minors, joined the Cleveland Indians in 1975. He was traded to Boston with Fred Kendall for catcher "Bo" Diaz, infielder Ted Cox, and pitchers Mike Paxton and Rick Wise, in March 1978. He stayed with the Red Sox until 1984 when he was traded by Boston along with Mike Brumley to the Cubs for Bill Buckner. He became a free agent but stayed with the Cubs. Later, in 1987, he was traded to Oakland for Dave Wilder. Dennis is one of the outstanding relief pitchers of the game. He was with Oakland in 1988 and pitched in two games in the World Series and was charged with one loss. He was also in one game in the 1989 World Series and was neither credited with a win nor charged with a loss. His lifetime record shows 165 victories and 138 defeats in 15 years. Rick pitched a no-run, no-hit game against the California Angels on May 30, 1977.

Woody English spent 10 years with the Cubs and two with Brooklyn. A shortstop and third baseman, Woody had a .286 life-time batting average. He played regularly with the Cubs from 1927 through 1936 and finished his career with Brooklyn in 1937 and 1938. Woody came from Fredonia, Ohio.

Johnny Evers, also called "The Crab," had a brother, Joe Evers, who played one game with the New York Giants. John came up with the Chicago Cubs in 1902 and stayed with them through 1913. He then went to the Boston Braves and later to the Philadelphia Phillies. He came to the White Sox in 1922, where he played in one game, and in 1929 he played in another game with the Boston Braves. In 18 years he had a batting average of .270 and was the middle man in the famous double-play combination, Tinkers-to-Evers-to-Chance. Johnny died in March 1947, in Albany, New

York. He was elected to baseball's Hall of Fame in 1946. Evers played in four World Series and batted .316 in them.

Dee Fondy was a left-handed first baseman who played with the Cubs from 1951 into 1957 when he went to Pittsburgh. He finished his career with Cincinnati in 1958. His eight-year batting average was .286 and he had 60 homeruns. From Slaton, Texas, Dee was traded by the Cubs to Pittsburgh in October 1950, along with Chuck Connors, in exchange for Hank Edwards and cash. When he returned to Chicago, Dee came with Gene Baker in exchange for Dale Long and Lee Walls.

Jimmy Foxx was one of the great sluggers of all time. He came from Sudlersville, Maryland, and joined the Philadelphia Athletics in 1925. He played there for 11 years and later went to the Boston Red Sox, the Chicago Cubs, and wound up his career with the Philadelphia Phillies. He was in the major leagues for 20 years and had a lifetime batting average of .325. He hit 534 homeruns and in 12 years he hit 30 or more. His best year was in 1932 when he hit 58 homers. He won the triple crown the following year when he repeated as Most Valuable Player and had a 50-homer season with the Red Sox in 1938. He died in July of 1967 in Miami, Florida, and entered the Hall of Fame in 1951.

Larry French pitched in the National League for 14 years. He started his career with Pittsburgh in 1929, came to the Cubs in 1935, and went to Brooklyn in 1941. He won 197 games and lost 171 during his 14-year career. He was in three World Series. In 1935 with the Cubs he lost two games, in 1938 (still with the Cubs) he had no decision, and he had no decision in the two games he pitched in for Brooklyn in 1941. His best year with the Cubs was 1936 when he won 18 and lost 9 games. He died in February 1987, in San Diego, California.

Jim Frey spent 16 years in the Baltimore Orioles system. He played professional baseball for 14 seasons but never made the big leagues. He won two batting titles in the minors and was Most

Shortstop Don Kessinger (1964–1969)

First baseman Phil Cavarretta (1934–1955)

Outfielder "Kiki" Cuyler (1928–1935)

Outfielder Hack Wilson (1926–1931)   Credit: NBL

Pitcher Charlie Root (1926–1941)

Pitcher "Big Ed" Reulbach (1905–1913)   Credit: Paul Thompson/NBL

1939 Chicago All-Stars, left to right: Second baseman Billy Herman (1931–1941); Catcher Gabby Hartnett (1922–1940); Pitcher "Big Bill" Lee (1934–1943, 1947); Third baseman Stan Hack (1932–1947)

Pitcher Rick Reuschel (1972–1981, 1983–1984)

Valuable Player with Tulsa in the Texas League when he played in the outfield there in 1957. Jim became general manager for the Cubs in 1988. He had managed the Cubs to the National League East Championship in 1984 and was named the Manager of the Year. He also managed the Cubs in 1985 and 1986 and had previously managed the Kansas City Royals in 1980 and part of 1981, winning the divisional championship in 1981, but losing the World Series to the Phillies. Jim attended Ohio State University.

Frank Frisch was called the "Fordham Flash." He attended Fordham University in New York and came to the Giants in 1919. He played in the major leagues for 19 years and accumulated a lifetime batting average of .316. He went to the Cardinals in 1927 and finished his career in 1937. He was in eight World Series and hit .294. Frank managed the Cardinals in 1934 when they won the World Series. After managing the Cardinals from 1933 through 1938, he then managed the Pittsburgh Pirates from 1940 through 1946 and the Chicago Cubs in 1949, 1950, and part of 1951. He went into baseball's Hall of Fame in 1947 and died in Wilmington, Delaware, in 1973.

Augie Galan was a switch-hitting outfielder from Berkley, California. He was the first National League player to hit two homeruns in one game, one batting right-handed, and one batting left-handed. He started out with the Cubs in 1934, went to Brooklyn in 1941, joined the Reds in 1947, and then went to the Giants in 1949. He wound up with the Philadelphia Athletics the same year. His 16-year career showed a batting average of .287 and he had an even 100 homeruns. He was in three World Series: in 1935 and 1938 with the Cubs and in 1941 with Brooklyn. He had a .138 average for the Series.

Joe Garagiola was a catcher who batted left-handed from St. Louis, Missouri. He was with the Cardinals from 1946 to 1951 and then went to Pittsburgh. He came to the Cubs in 1953 and played there part of 1954 before joining the Giants. He finished his nine-year career with a lifetime batting average of .257. He was in the

World Series in 1946 with the Cardinals and batted .316. In one game he got four hits in four times at bat. Joe is well known for his great broadcasting ability, and great witticisms.

Mark Grace, a left-handed batter who also throws left-handed, hails from Winston-Salem, North Carolina. After three years in the minors he came up to the Cubs in 1988 and batted .296 with seven homeruns. He hit .314 in 1989 with 13 homeruns, giving him, for his two years in the big leagues, an average of .305 and a total of 20 homeruns. In the championship playoffs in 1989, Mark went to bat 17 times; got 11 hits, including three doubles, a triple, and a homerun; drove in eight runs; had a .640 average; and was outstanding in the field.

Burleigh Grimes pitched in the National League for 19 years. He won 270 games and lost 212. He was a spitball pitcher and won 20 games or more on five different occasions. He pitched for Pittsburgh, Brooklyn, the Giants, the Cardinals, and the Cubs. He entered baseball's Hall of Fame in 1964 and died in December 1985, in Clear Lake, Wisconsin.

Charlie Grimm, "Jolly Cholly," played in the National League for 20 years. A left-handed first baseman, he was with the Cubs for 12 years. He managed the Cubs from 1932 to 1949, the Boston Braves in 1952, and again in 1953 through 1956 when they moved to Milwaukee, and returned to manage the Cubs again in 1960. He was in three World Series as a manager: in 1932, when the Cubs lost to the Yankees in four straight; in 1935, when the Cubs lost to the Tigers in six games; and again in 1945, when the Cubs lost to the Tigers in seven games. Charlie had a .290 lifetime batting average for his 20 years in the big leagues. As a player in two World Series, he hit .364. He originally came from St. Louis, Missouri, and he died in November 1983, in Scottsdale, Arizona.

Stan Hack from Sacramento, California, played for 16 years (1932–1947) at third base for the Chicago Cubs. He was a left-handed batter, who threw right-handed. Stan was in four World

Series with the Cubs and hit .348 in those Series. His lifetime batting average for his 16 years in the big leagues was .301. He managed the Cubs in 1954, 1955, and 1956, and the St. Louis Cardinals for part of 1958. Stan died in 1979 in Dixon, Illinois.

Warren Hacker came from Marissa, Illinois. He was a right-handed pitcher who was with the Cubs from 1948 to 1957, and then went to the Reds, the Phillies, and the White Sox. In 12 years he won 62 and lost 89 ballgames. His best year was 1952 when he won 15 and lost nine.

Bill Hands was a right-handed pitcher from Hackensack, New Jersey, who started his career in the majors with San Francisco in 1965. He came to the Cubs in 1966 and stayed there until 1973, when he went to Minnesota. He later went to Texas and was in the big leagues for 11 years, winning 111 games and losing 110. In 1969 he was a 20-game winner, losing 14; he won 18 games an lost 15 in 1970.

Gabby Hartnett caught for the Chicago Cubs for 19 years and then spent his 20th year with the New York Giants. He had a .297 lifetime batting average. He managed the team in 1938, 1939, and 1940. In his first year of managing the Cubs, Gabby hit a memorable homerun in near darkness to beat the Pirates and lead the Cubs to the pennant in 1938. Gabby died in Park Ridge, Illinois, in December of 1972. He entered baseball's Hall of Fame in 1955.

Cliff Heathcote was a left-handed hitting and throwing outfielder from Glen Rock, Pennsylvania. He came up to the big leagues in 1918 with the Cardinals, then came over to the Cubs in 1922 and stayed with them until 1931. He finished his career in 1932 with the Cincinnati Reds and the Philadelphia Phillies. In his 15-year career Cliff had a lifetime batting average of .275. He was in the World Series in 1929, made one appearance at the plate, and failed to get a hit. He died on January 19, 1939, in York, Pennsylvania.

149

Billy Herman was the Cubs' second baseman from 1931 to the middle of 1941. He then went to Brooklyn, later to the Boston Braves, and finally to the Pittsburgh Pirates in 1947. He had a lifetime batting average of .304. In four World Series he hit .242. Billy later managed the Pittsburgh Pirates in 1947 and the Boston Red Sox in 1964, 1965, and 1966. He was inducted into baseball's Hall of Fame in 1975.

Jim Hickman was a right-handed hitting and right-handed throwing outfielder who started off with the New York Mets in 1962. He went to Los Angeles in 1967 and came to the Cubs in 1968, where he stayed until 1974 when he went to the Cardinals. His 13-year batting average was .252 and he hit 159 homeruns. Jim was from Henning, Tennessee.

Charlie Hollocher came from St. Louis, Missouri, and was the Cubs' regular shortstop from 1918 until 1922. He finished with the Cubs in 1924, and his 7-year batting average was .304. He was in one World Series in 1918. Charlie died in 1940 in Frontenac, Missouri.

Ken Holtzman spent 15 years in the big leagues. He was a left-handed pitcher from St. Louis, Missouri. Ken started his career with the Chicago Cubs in 1965 and played there through 1971. He was traded to Oakland on November 29, 1971, for Rick Monday. He pitched for Oakland until 1976 when he went to Baltimore in a trade with Reggie Jackson and Bill Vanbommel. In exchange, they received Don Baylor, Mike Torrez, and Paul Mitchell. Two months later he was traded to the Yankees in another block-buster deal. Doyle Alexander, Grant Jackson, Ellie Hendricks, and Jimmy Freeman went to New York with Holtzman in exchange for Rudy May, Tippy Martinez, Dave Pagan, Scott McGregor, and Rick Dempsey. He stayed with the Yankees until 1978 when he came back to the Cubs and finished his career in 1979. Ken won 174 games and lost 150 in his 15-year career. In World Series play he won four games and lost one. He was with Oakland in 1972, 1973, and 1974 when they won the pennant and the World Series. Ken did

150

a good job with the bat in the World Series, going to bat 12 times and getting four hits for a .333 average. One of them was a homerun.

Burt Hooton, or "Happy" as he was called by his teammates, came up with the Cubs in 1971. He was a right-handed pitcher from Greenville, Texas. He stayed with the Cubs until 1975 when he went with the Los Angeles Dodgers in exchange for Geoff Zahn and Eddie Solomon. He was with the Dodgers until 1985 when he went to Texas. In his 15 years in the big leagues, he won 151 games and lost 136. His best year was 1978 when he won 19 and lost 10. In the World Series in 1977, 1978, and 1981, with Los Angeles, he won three games and lost three.

Rogers Hornsby played 23 years in the big leagues, mainly with the St. Louis Cardinals, and later with the New York Giants, the Boston Braves, Chicago Cubs, the Cardinals again, and then the St. Louis Browns. He had a lifetime batting average of .358 and was a second baseman. Three times he hit over .400. He led the National League in batting on seven different occasions. He managed the St. Louis Cardinals in 1925 and 1926; the Boston Braves in 1928; the Cubs in 1930, 1931, and 1932; and the St. Louis Browns from 1933 to 1937 and again for part of 1952. He also managed the Cincinnati Reds in 1952 and 1953. Rogers died on January 5, 1963, in Chicago, Illinois. He entered baseball's Hall of Fame in 1942.

Kenny Hubbs came from Riverside, California. He was a right-handed, batting second baseman who played three years with the Cubs, batting .247. An excellent fielder, he was killed in a Provo, Utah airplane accident in 1974 at the age of 22.

Monte Irvin played with the New York Giants from 1949 through 1955. He finished his career with the Chicago Cubs in 1956. Monte was best known for his play in the Negro Leagues before he came up to the Giants in 1949. He batted .458 and stole home in the 1951 World Series against the Yankees. He had a lifetime batting average of .293 and was admitted to baseball's Hall of Fame in 1973.

Chatham, Ontario, in Canada furnished the big leagues with **Ferguson Jenkins.** He was a right-handed pitcher and lasted for 19 years, winning 284 games and losing 226. He started out with the Phillies and came to the Cubs in 1966. He stayed with the Cubs through 1973, then went to Texas, to Boston, back to Texas, and then back to the Cubs. He won 20 or more games on seven occasions, six of them in a row. He won 25 games in 1974 and lost 12. He won 24 in 1971 and lost 13. He was an excellent pitcher and deserves to be in baseball's Hall of Fame.

Bill Jurges, who came up with the Cubs in 1931, was one of the finer shortstops of his day. He played shortstop there through 1938. After the 1938 season he was traded with Frank Demaree and Ken O'Dea for Dick Bartell, Hank Leiber, and Gus Mancuso to the New York Giants. He spent seven years with the Giants and returned to the Cubs in 1946, where he finished his career in 1947. His 17-year career record showed a .258 batting average. In three World Series (1932, 1935, and 1938, all with the Cubs), he went to bat 40 times and got 11 hits for a .275 average. He managed the Boston Red Sox for the last half of the season in 1959 and the first half of the season in 1960.

Tony Kaufmann joined the Cubs in 1921 at the end of the season. He pitched for Chicago from 1922 until the middle of 1927, when he was sent to the Phillies. He finished the 1927 season with the St. Louis Cardinals, pitched there in 1928, went to the Giants in 1929, and returned to the Cardinals for 1930, 1931, and 1935. In his 12 years he won 64 games and lost 62. His best year was with the Cubs in 1924, when he won 16 and lost 11. He won 14 games in 1923 and 13 games in 1925. Tony died in June 1982 in Elgin, Illinois.

Vic Keen won 15 ballgames pitching for the Cubs in 1924. (He had won 12 in 1923.) Vic pitched for the Cubs from 1921 to 1926,

152

then went to the Cardinals, where he won 10 and lost 9 in 1926. He had started his career with the Philadelphia Athletics, pitching in one game in 118. His eight-year career record showed 42 wins and 44 losses. In the World Series in 1926 he was in one game and had no decision. Vic died in December 1976, at Salisbury, Maryland.

George "Highpockets" Kelly was a first baseman in the National League playing with the New York Giants, Pittsburgh Pirates, Cincinnati Reds, Chicago Cubs, and Brooklyn Dodgers. He played 16 years with a lifetime batting average of .297. He was in four World Series, all with the Giants, and hit .248. Noted as an outstanding fielder, he died on October 13, 1984, in Burlingame, California. He was admitted to baseball's Hall of Fame in 1973.

Mike Kelly, who was better known as "King," was one of the greatest players of his time. He played in the old National League, starting with Cincinnati in 1878. He was with Chicago from 1889 through 1886 and wound up his career n 1893 with New York in the National League. He had a lifetime batting average of .307 for 16 years. One of the great base runners of all time, he inspired his fans to coin the battle cry, "Slide, Kelly, slide!" He died in 1894 in Boston, Massachusetts, and was named to baseball's Hall of Fame in 1945.

Don Kessinger was a switch-hitting shortstop who came up with the Chicago Cubs in 1964 and stayed there through 1975. He played with the Cardinals in 1976 and part of 1977, and spent the rest of his career with the White Sox, finishing up in 1979, as both player and manager. His 16-year career showed a batting average of .252. Don came from Forrest City, Arkansas.

Bill Killefer was in the major leagues for 13 years. From Bloomingdale, Michigan, Bill was a catcher and batted right-handed. He started out with the St. Louis Browns in 1909, went to the Phillies in the National League in 1911, and stayed there until 1918 when he went with the Cubs. He finished his major league career as a player in 1921. His 13-year batting average was .238. Bill was in two World Series, in 1915 with the Phillies and 1918 with the Cubs. He went to bat 18 times and got two hits for a .111 batting average. In 1921 he took over the managerial position with the Cubs. He managed the Cubs through 1925 and in 1930, 1931, 1932, and 1933 he managed the St. Louis Browns. Bill died in Elsmere, Delaware, in July, 1960.

Ralph Kiner was a right-handed hitter, with the Pittsburgh Pirates from 1946 to 1953, when he went with the Cubs. He played with the Cubs through 1954, and then wound up his 10-year career with the Cleveland Indians in 1955. He had a lifetime batting average of .279 and hit 369 homeruns. Ralph won the homerun title or shared it in each of his first seven years with Pittsburgh. He is now a broadcaster in New York. He was elected to the Hall of Fame in 1975.

Dave Kingman from Pendleton, Oregon, was given the nickname "King Kong." He was a right-handed batter who put in 16 years in the major leagues and had a lifetime batting average of .236 with 442 homeruns. He led the National League in homeruns in 1979 with 48 and again in 1982 with 37. He led the National League in runs batted in in 1979 with 131 and led it again in 1981 with 105, and again in 1982 with 156. Dave came into the majors in 1971 with the San Francisco Giants. He went to the Mets in 1975; in 1977 he started out the season with the Mets, went to San Diego, then to California, and then to the Yankees. He came to the Chicago Cubs in 1978 and played there for three years. He went back with the Mets in 1981, stayed there until 1984, and then spent the last three years, (1984, 1985 and 1986) with Oakland.

Chuck Klein had a 17-year career in the major leagues, starting out with the Philadelphia Phillies. He then went to the Cubs, back to the Phillies, then to Pittsburgh, and back again to the Phillies. He had a lifetime batting average of .320 and hit an even 300 homeruns during his 17 years. He was in one World Series in 1935 when the Cubs were defeated by the Tigers. He led the National League in batting in 1933, hitting .368, and led the League in runs

154

batted in in 1931 and 1933. Chuck died on March 23, 1958, in Indianapolis, Indiana. He entered baseball's Hall of Fame in 1980.

Mark Koenig is the only ballplayer still alive who played with the Yankees in 1927. The Yankees of 1927 have always been considered the greatest ball club of all time. A switch-hitting shortstop, Mark was with the Yankees from 1925 to 1930, when he came to the Detroit Tigers along with Waite Hoyt in a trade for Owen Carroll, George Wuestling, and Harry Rice. He stayed with the Tigers through the 1931 season and then went to the Cubs in 1932. He was with the Cubs in the World Series of 1932, when Babe Ruth and the other Yankees taunted the Cubs about being cheap because they had left off Rogers Hornsby from the World Series money. Hornsby had managed the club the first half of the season and the rest of the Yankees kept taunting the Cubs and saying to Koenig, "Why don't you come back and belong with a good ball club instead of those cheapskates?" Mark went to the Reds after the 1933 season and then with the Giants in 1935 and 1936. In 12 years he had a .279 lifetime batting average.

Dennis Lamp was a right-handed pitcher who started his major league career with the Cubs in 1977. In 1981 he went to the White Sox and in 1984, Toronto. He finished his 11-year career with Oakland in 1987. Dennis won 75 games and lost 79. His best year was in 1985 when he won 11 games for Toronto and didn't lose any. He was used mainly as a relief pitcher, starting only 162 games in the entire 11 years.

Les Lancaster is a right-handed pitcher from Dallas, Texas. He joined the Cubs in 1987, when he won eight and lost three games. In 1988 he won four and lost six. In 1989 he won four and lost two, giving him 16 wins and 11 losses in his three years in the big time. In the Championship Series of 1989 he pitched in six innings in two games and was credited with one victory and charged with one loss.

155

Vance Law came from Boise, Idaho. He is the son of Vern Law, who pitched for many years in the majors. Vance is a right-handed hitting and throwing infielder who started with Pittsburgh in 1980. He came to the White Sox in 1982, went to Montreal in 1985, and came to the Cubs in 1988. He has a lifetime batting average of .257. In the playoffs of 1989 he was used three times as a pinch-hitter and failed to get a hit.

Tony LaRussa was a right-handed hitting shortstop second baseman who came from Tampa, Florida. He was in the American League for six years, playing in only 132 games. He had a batting average of .199. Tony started with Kansas City in 1963, and played for Oakland in 1968, 1979, 1970 and part of 1971, when he went to Atlanta. In 1973 he was in one game for the Chicago Cubs. He managed the White Sox from 1979 to mid 1986. He then started managing the Oakland A's, taking them to the pennant in 1988 and in 1989 to a four-game sweep of the San Francisco Giants in the World Series.

Bill Lee came from Plaquemine, Louisiana. He was a right-handed pitcher who came up with the Cubs in 1934. He stayed with the Cubs until 1943 when he went to the Philadelphia Phillies. In 1945, he went to the Boston Braves and came back to the Cubs in 1947. He had a 14-year career with 169 wins and 157 losses. In 1935 he won 20 games and lost six, having the highest percentage of any pitcher in the National League. He did that again in 1938, when he won 22 and lost nine. He won 19 and lost 15 in 1939, and in 1936 he won 18 and lost 11. He died in his hometown in June of 1977.

Fred Lindstrom, at 18 years old, was the youngest player to appear in World Series, which he did with the New York Giants in 1924. He got four hits in the fifth game against the Senators and batted .333 for the seven games. Fred had seven .300 seasons and twice guarded 231 hits. His lifetime batting average was .311. He played with the Giants from 1924 through 1932, with Pittsburgh in 1933 and 1934, with the Cubs in 1935, and with Brooklyn in 1936. He later coached at Northwestern University in Evanston, Illinois.

Fred died in October of 1981 in Chicago. He was admitted to baseball's Hall of Fame in 1976.

Turk Lown came from Brooklyn, New York and was a relief pitcher in the major leagues for 11 years. He started with the Cubs in 1951, went on to Cincinnati in 1958, and then to the White Sox, where he spent the next four years. He won 55 games and lost 61, lifetime. He was used almost entirely as a relief pitcher. Turk was in the World Series of 1959, with three games and no decisions.

"Peanuts" Lowrey came from Culver City, California. He was a right-handed hitting and throwing outfielder. He joined the Cubs in 1942, and played there until 1949 when he went to the Reds. In 1950 he went to the Cardinals and stayed with them through 1954. In 1955 he wound up with the Philadelphia Phillies. He had a 13-year career, batting .273 lifetime and hitting 37 homeruns. In the World Series of 1945 against the Detroit Tigers, Peanuts batted 29 times and got nine hits for a .310 average. He died in July 1986 in Inglewood, California.

Greg Maddux is the brother of Mike Maddux, who pitched for the Phillies. He joined the Cubs in 1986 and pitched there in 1987 and in 1988, winning 18 games and losing eight. In 1989 he won 19 and lost 12, giving him 45 victories and 38 defeats in his four years with the Cubs. In the playoffs he pitched 7 1/3 innings and was the losing pitcher in one game.

Bill Madlock was right-handed hitting and throwing, mainly third base. He also played a little at second and first. He started in the big leagues in 1973 with Texas and came to the Cubs in 1974. In 1977 he went with San Francisco, and in 1979 he went to Pittsburgh, staying until 1985 when he went with the Dodgers. Two years later, he went to the Detroit Tigers. Bill played 15 years in the majors and had a lifetime batting average of .305. He led the league in batting in 1975 and 1976 and in 1981 and 1983, four times in all. He was in the World Series with Pittsburgh in 1979, went to bat 24 times, and got nine hits, hitting .375. He was known as "Mad Dog."

Pat Malone was a right-handed pitcher who came from Altoona, Pennsylvania. He started his major league career with the Cubs in 1928, winning 18 games and losing 13. In 1929 he won 22 and lost 10. In 1930 he won 20 and lost nine. He stayed with the Cubs through 1934, winning no more than 16 games after 1930. He went to the Yankees in 1935 and spent three seasons with them. In his ten years in the majors, Pat won 134 games and lost 92. He was in three, losing 2 games in 1929 when the Cubs played the Philadelphia Athletics. In 1932 he was in one game but with no decision. In 1936 with the Yankees he was charged with one defeat. He died in May of 1943 in his native Altoona, Pennsylvania.

"Rabbit" Maranville played for 23 years in the National League, starting out with Boston, going to Pittsburgh, then to the Cubs, on to Brooklyn, then to the Cards, and back again with Boston. He had a lifetime batting average of .258 and was in two World Series (1914 and 1928). He was a small player (5'5") and weighed about 155 pounds. He was a shortstop, an excellent fielder, and an outstanding clutch performer. A member of the 1914 Miracle Braves, he managed the Chicago Cubs briefly in 1925. He died in January of 1954 in New York City and entered baseball's Hall of Fame the same year.

Marty Marion was one of the great fielding shortstops of all time. He batted and threw right-handed and played for the St. Louis Cards for 11 years and two for the St. Louis Browns. He came up with the Cardinals in 1940 and played there through 1950. He then played with the Browns in 1952 and 1953 briefly. He had a lifetime batting average of .263 and 36 homeruns and played in four World Series with the Cardinals (1942, 1943, 1944, and 1946). He batted .231, getting 18 hits and 78 times at bat. Marty had a brother, Red Marion, who played for two years with Washington. Marty managed the Cardinals in 1951 and the Browns in 1952 and 1953. He also managed the White Sox in 1954, 1955, and 1956.

158

Gary Matthews, who came from San Fernando, California, was a right-handed hitting outfielder and also threw right-handed. He spent 16 years in the big leagues, coming up with San Francisco in 1972. He went to Atlanta in 1977, staying until 1981 when he went to the Phillies, where he played 1981, 1982, and 1983. He then came to the Cubs in 1984 and went to Seattle in 1987. He was a long ball hitter, having 234 homeruns in his 16-year career and a batting average of .281. In the 1983 World Series with the Phillies he went to bat 16 times and got four hits for a .250 batting average.

Joe McCarthy did not play in the big leagues but he managed for 24 seasons (the Cubs from 1926 through 1930, the Yankees from 1931 into 1946, and the Boston Red Sox in 1948, 1949, and 1950). He was considered one of the all-time great managers. His team won nine pennants and seven World Series. Joe died in Buffalo in 1978. He entered baseball's Hall of Fame in 1957.

Clyde McCullough came out of Nashville, Tennessee. He was a right-handed hitting catcher who had a 15-year career in the major leagues and a lifetime batting average of .252 with 52 homeruns in his 15 years. He started out with the Cubs in 1940 and stayed with them through 1948. He was with the Pirates from 1949 to 1953, when he came back with the Cubs. He retired in 1956 and died in San Francisco in September of 1982. He is the only man ever to get into a World Series game without having played in any regular games. He was in the service in 1945 and came out in time to appear in one game in the Series.

Fred Merkle came from Watertown, Wisconsin. He was a right-handed batter and threw right-handed. He played first base in the National League for 14 years with the Giants, Dodgers, and Cubs, and finished his career in two seasons with the New York Yankees in 1925 and 1926. With a lifetime batting average of .273, he played in five World Series, batting .239 and getting 21 hits in 88 times at bat. His famous boner is described in another part of this book. Fred died in Daytona Beach, Florida, in 1956.

159

Lennie Merulo came up with the Cubs in 1941 and played through 1947. He was the regular shortstop most of the time. In his seven years he had a lifetime batting average of .240. In the 1945 World Series he went to bat twice and failed to get a hit. He hit only six homeruns during his seven-year career. Lennie hailed from Boston, Massachusetts, and was right-handed all the way.

Eddie Miksis came from Burlington, New Jersey. He threw right-handed and batted right-handed. He was an infielder but sometimes played in the outfield. He came up with Brooklyn in 1944 and played there until June 15, 1951, when he was traded with Bruce Edwards, Joe Hatten, and Gene Hermanski to the Cubs for Johnny Schmitz, Rube Walker, Andy Pafko, and Wayne Terwilliger. Eddie played for the Cubs from 1951 on. Then in 1957 he went to the Cardinals, later to Baltimore, and wound up his career with Cincinnati in 1958. During 1955 he played most of the time in the infield. His 14-year batting average was .236. Eddie was in two World Series with Brooklyn in 1947 and 1949. He went to bat 11 times and got 3 hits for a .273 batting average.

Paul Minner, who was called "Lefty," came from New Wilmington, Pennsylvania. A left-handed pitcher, he started his big league career with Brooklyn in 1946. He came to the Cubs in 1950 along with Preston Ward in a cash deal. He pitched for the Cubs from 1950 through 1956. His best year was 1952, when he won 14 and lost nine. He had two other years when he won more than 10 games (1953 when he won 12 and 1954 when he won 11). His major league career shows 60 wins and 84 losses. He was in the World Series in 1949, pitching for Brooklyn. He pitched in one game and was neither credited with a win nor charged with a loss.

Rick Monday was a left-handed hitting outfielder who also threw left-handed. He came up to Kansas City in 1966, went to Oakland in 1968, and came to the Cubs in 1972. He played with the Cubs for five years, then went to the Los Angeles Dodgers, and played there from 1977 through 1984. In his major league career of 19 years he had a lifetime batting average of .264 along with 241 homeruns. He was in three World Series (1977, 1978, and 1981) with the Dodgers. He went to bat 38 times in those three series and batted .184 with only seven hits.

Keith Moreland came from Dallas, Texas. He was a right-handed batter and threw right-handed. He played mainly in the outfield, occasionally at third base, sometimes caught, and also played first base. He came up with the Phillies in 1978 and joined the Cubs in 1982. He was with San Diego in 1988, went to the Tigers in 1989, and was later traded to Baltimore for Brian DuBois. He announced his retirement after the 1989 season. He has a life-time average of .279 with 121 homeruns. Keith had spent 12 years in the major leagues. He was in one World Series with the Phillies in 1980, got four hits in 12 times at bat, for a .333 average.

Billy Nicholson, or "Swish," was a left-handed batter who threw right-handed. He came up to the Philadelphia Phillies in 1936 and then went back to the minors. He joined the Cubs in 1939 and played with them through 1948. He went back to the Phillies in 1949 and finished his major league career with the Phillies in 1953. He was a powerful hitter, hitting 25 or more homeruns on 6 occasions. He led the league in homers in 1944 with 33 and in 1943 with 29. He also led the league in runs batted in those two years, having 128 in 1943 and 122 in 1944. He had 235 homeruns in his career, with a lifetime batting average of .268. Billy was in the World Series against the Detroit Tigers in 1945. He went to bat 28 times and got 6 hits for a .214 average.

Bob Nieman is the only player in major league history to hit two homeruns in his first two times at bat, which he did in 1951 with the St. Louis Browns. Although he went to bat 43 times that year, those were the only two homeruns that he had. He later played with the White Sox in 1955.

Lou Novikoff was called the "Mad Russian." He was a very colorful ballplayer who played with the Cubs from 1941 through 1944. He was with the Phillies in 1946. His five-year career showed a batting average of .282 and 15 homeruns. He came from Glendale, Arizona, and died in September of 1970 in South Gate, California.

Ken O'Dea was a left-handed hitting catcher who came from Lima, New York. He joined the majors in 1935 with the Chicago Cubs and played with them for four years. He went to the New York Giants in 1939 and then to the Cardinals in 1942. He wound up his career with the Boston Braves in 1946. He had a 12-year career with a .255 batting average and 40 homeruns. Ken was in five World Series, went to bat 13 times total, and had six hits for a .462 batting average. Ken died in his hometown of Lima, New York in December 1985.

Bob O'Farrell spent 21 years in the major leagues as a catcher. A right-handed hitter and thrower, he joined the Cubs in 1915 and played with them into 1925 when he went to the St. Louis Cardinals. He was with the Cardinals in 1926 and 1927 and managed the team in 1927. He also managed the Cincinnati Reds during part of the 1934 season. He stayed there until 1933 when he went back to the Cardinals. He then went to Cincinnati, back to the Cubs, and then back again to the Cardinals. He had a lifetime batting average of .273 and hit 51 homeruns. He was in the World Series in 1918 with the Cubs and in 1926 with the Cardinals. He had seven hits in 26 times at bat for a .269 batting average. Bob came from Waukegan, Illinois.

Andy Pafko, or "Handy Andy" as he was known, was a right-handed hitter who threw right-handed and came from Boyceville, Wisconsin. He joined the Cubs in 1943 and stayed with them into 1951 when he went to Brooklyn. He went to Milwaukee in 1953 and finished his career with the Milwaukee Braves in 1959. He had 17 years in the majors and had a batting average of .285. He was an excellent centerfielder. He played in the World Series of 1945 with the Cubs, 1952 with Brooklyn, and 1957 and 1958 with Milwaukee. He had 16 hits in 72 times at bat in those four World Series for a .222 average.

162

Milt Pappas came from Detroit, Michigan. He was a right-handed pitcher who first joined the Baltimore Orioles in 1957 and played with them through 1965. In December of 1965 he was traded to Cincinnati with Jack Baldschun and Dick Simpson for Frank Robinson, a trade that Baltimore will always love the Reds for. Milt stayed with the Reds until 1968 when he went to Atlanta. He came to the Cubs in 1970 and stayed until the end of 1973. In his 17 years he won 209 ballgames and lost 169. He pitched a no-run, no-hit game on September 2, 1972, against the San Diego Padres as the Cubs won 8-0. He had a perfect game going until two men were out in the ninth when he lost a questionable call and walked Larry Stahl. Milt is now a resident of suburban Chicago.

Claude Passeau came from Waynesboro, Mississippi. He was a right-handed pitcher who first joined Pittsburgh in 1935, went to the Phillies in 1936, and came to the Cubs in 1939. He pitched for the Cubs from 1939 through 1947. In his 13-year career he won 162 ballgames and lost 150. He won 20 ballgames in 1940, losing only 13. He won 19 in 1942, 17 in 1945, and three times won a total of 15 (1939, 1943 and 1944). In the World Series of 1945 he pitched a one-hit ballgame, Rudy York getting the only hit as the Cubs bested the Tigers that day. It was his only appearance in a World Series.

"The Vulture" was the nickname of **Phil Regan**, who pitched for 13 years in the major leagues. He came up with the Tigers in 1960 and went to Lost Angeles in 1966 in a trade for Dick Tracewski. He pitched for Los Angeles for two years and went to the Cubs in 1968. In 1972 he went to the Cubs. He was primarily a relief pitcher. His best year, though, was as a starting pitcher with the Tigers in 1963 when he won 15 games. In 1966 he won 14 games while being charged with a defeat only once — all in relief — when he was with the Los Angeles Dodgers. With the Cubs in 1969 and 1970, he pitched in over 70 ballgames, winning 12 in 1969 and five in 1970. He won 96 games in his 13-year career and lost 81. He was credited with 92 saves. He had a brief appearance in the 1966 World Series when Los Angeles was beaten in four straight games by

Baltimore. He was in two games and had no decision. After his baseball career, Phil coached baseball at Grand Valley.

"Big Ed" Reulbach, who came from Detroit, Michigan, was a right-hander who joined the Chicago Cubs in 1905. He played with them into the middle of 1913 when he went with Brooklyn. He was in the Federal League in 1915 and wound up his major league career with the Boston Braves in 1917. He was in the majors for 13 years and won 181 games and lost 105. In 1906 he won 19 and lost four, and in 1907 he won 17 and lost four. He won 24 and lost seven in 1908, and won 19 games in 1909. Each year he led the league with the highest winning percentage. When he was in the Federal League, he won 20 and lost 10. Big Ed was in four World Series with the Cubs (in 1906, 1907, 1908, and 1910). He was credited with two victories and no defeats. He died in 1961 in Glens Falls, New York.

Rick Reuschel is a right-handed pitcher who came from Quincy, Illinois. He started in the minors in 1970 and came up with the Cubs in 1972. He stayed with the Cubs until 1981 when he was traded to the New York Yankees for Doug Bird and Mike Griffin. He was with the Yankees in 1981 and 1982. In 1983 he went back to the minors, but he came back to the Cubs in 1983 and 1984. He went to Hawaii in the Pacific Coast League in 1985 and he was with Pittsburgh in 1985, 1986, and 1987, before being traded to San Francisco in 1987 for Jeff Robinson and Scott Medvin. He was with the Giants in 1988 and 1989. He has won 211 games and lost 181 in his 17 years in the big leagues. In 1981 he was with the Yankees in two games of the World Series. He had no decision. In the playoffs of 1989 he was in two games, won one game and lost one.

For 17 years **Charlie Root** pitched in the major leagues, 16 of them with the Chicago Cubs. He started his career with the Browns in 1923, went back to the minors, and came up to the Cubs in 1926 to stay. He won 26 games in 1927, the most any pitcher did that year. He had the highest winning percentage in 1929 when he won

19 games and lost six. Charlie was from Middletown, Ohio. He won 201 games during his career and lost 160. He was in four World Series : 1929, 1932, 1935, and 1938. He was not credited with a win and was charged with a loss three times. Charlie died in Hollister, California, in November of 1970.

From the "Cereal Capital of the World," Battle Creek, Michigan, came **Bob Rush**, a right-handed pitcher who joined the Cubs in 1948. He was with them through 1957 when he went to Milwaukee, and in 1960 he finished his 13-year career with the White Sox. He won 127 games and lost 152 in his 13 years. He was with Milwaukee in 1958 in the World Series and was charged with a defeat and not credited with a win. Bob's best year was 1952, when he won 17 and lost 13. In 1950 he lost 20 ballgames, the most of any pitcher in the league, and he won 13.

Ryne Sandberg, one of the outstanding second basemen of this era, has been with the Cubs since 1982. He played four years in the minor leagues and came up with the Phillies in 1981. He was traded to the Cubs along with Larry Bowa for Ivan DeJesus in January 1982. Ryne was named the Most Valuable Player in the National League in 1984. He has a lifetime batting average of .285 for his nine years in the big show. He has hit 139 homeruns. In the championship series of 1989 Ryne had eight hits at 20 times at bat for a .400 average, which is slightly better than he had in 1984 during the championship series when he hit .368 with seven hits in 19 times at bat.

Scott Sanderson is a right-handed pitcher from Dearborn, Michigan. He came up with Montreal in 1978 and stayed there until 1984 when he went with the Cubs. He has been with the Cubs ever since. He won 11 and lost nine in 1989, bringing his record up to 98 wins and 89 losses in 12 years. In the playoffs of 1989 he pitched in one game, two innings, and was neither credited with a win or charged with a loss.

Ron Santo came up with the Cubs in 1960 and was their regular third baseman through the 1973 season. He played then with the White Sox in 1974, giving him 15 years in the majors in which he amassed a .277 lifetime batting average along with 342 homeruns. He was also a fielding wizard. Four times during his career he hit 30 homeruns or more. Ron is a native of Seattle, Washington.

Hank Sauer came from Pittsburgh, Pennsylvania. He had a brother, Ed, who played for the Cubs in 1943, 1944, and 1945. Hank was an outfielder, starting his career in 1941 with Cincinnati. He came to the Cubs in 1949 and played there through 1955. He then went to the Cards and wound up with the Giants during the last three years of his career. In 15 years Hank had a .266 lifetime batting average and hit 288 homeruns.

Bob Scheffing came from Overland, Missouri. He joined the Cubs in 1941, played with them in 1942, came back after the war in 1946, and played through 1949. He went to Cincinnati in the middle of the 1950 season and finished his career with Cincinnati and St. Louis Cardinals in 1951. He was a right-handed hitting catcher. His eight-year career showed a .263 batting average. He managed the Cubs in 1957, 1958, and 1959, and managed the Detroit Tigers in 1961, nearly winning the pennant that year. He managed them also in 1962 and was replaced in the middle of the 1963 season. Bob died in Phoenix, Arizona in October of 1985.

Johnny Schmitz was called "Bear Tracks." He was a right-handed batter but a left-handed pitcher. He joined the Cubs in 1941 and was with them until 1951, except for the war years. He then went to Brooklyn, the Yankees, the Reds, the Yankees again, the Senators, the Red Sox, and Baltimore. His 13-year career showed 93 wins and 114 losses. In 1947 he won 13 and lost 18 for the Cubs; he reversed that in 1948, winning 18 and losing 13. That was Johnny's best season. John was a native of Wausau, Wisconsin.

Frank Schulte was called nothing but "Wildfire." He was a left-handed hitter, threw right-handed, and was an outfielder. He came

166

from Cohocton, New York, and he joined the Chicago Cubs in 1904, staying with them until 1916 when he went to Pittsburgh. Then he went to the Phillies and to Washington. He spent 15 years in the major leagues, and had a lifetime batting average of .270. He was in four World Series and hit .309 in those games.

Frank Secory came from Mason City, Iowa. He was an outfielder, batted right, and threw right. He played in one game with the Detroit Tigers in 1940. In 1942 he was with the Cincinnati Reds, and in 1944, 1945, and 1946 with the Cubs. In five years he had a lifetime batting average of .228 with seven homeruns. He was in the World Series in 1945, playing for the Cubs against the Tigers. He went to bat five times and got two hits for a .400 average. Frank umpired in the National League for 18 years after his major league career ended. Frank is a member of three Halls of Fame: Muskegon, Michigan Area Sports Hall of Fame; Western Michigan University Hall of Fame; and Port Huron Hall of Fame. Frank now resides in Port Huron, Michigan.

Bill Serenk came from Alameda, California. He was a right-handed hitting third baseman who played for six years with the Cubs. He had a batting average of .251 and had a total of 48 homeruns. Bill played from 1949 through 1954.

Roy Smalley came from Springfield, Missouri. He was a right-handed hitting shortstop. He played with the Cubs from 1948 through 1953. He went to Milwaukee in 1954 and to the Phillies in 1955. He finished his career with the Phillies in 1958. His 11-year batting average was .227, and he had a total of 61 homeruns. Roy is the father of Roy Smalley, Jr., who has had a long career in the American League with Texas, Minnesota, the Yankees, and the White Sox.

Lee Smith came out of Jamestown, Louisiana. He joined the Cubs in 1980 and pitched with them through 1987. In 1988 he went with the Boston Red Sox. His nine-year career showed 60 victories and 57 losses. He has been used almost entirely as a relief pitcher,

167

starting only six games. He started five times in 1982 and once in 1981. All the rest of his 586 ballgames were in relief.

Jigger Statz was a switch-hitting outfielder who joined the Giants in 1919, went to the Red Sox in 1920, and came to the Cubs in 1922. He played four years with the Cubs and then went to Brooklyn, where he finished his eight-year career in 1928. He had a long minor league career after that in the Pacific Coast League. His batting average in the major leagues was .285. Jigger, as he was known, was a native of Waukegan, Illinois.

Harry Steinfeldt is probably best known as the answer to that great trivia question, "Who was the third baseman in the Tinkers-to-Evers-to-Chance infield?" Harry played with the Cubs in 1906 through 1910, which were the heydays of the Tinkers-to-Evers-to-Chance trio. He started his career in 1898 with Cincinnati and came to the Cubs in 1906. He finished his 14-year career with the Boston Braves in 1911. He had a .268 batting average and hit 27 homeruns during his career. He was in four World Series with the Cubs: in 1906, 1907, 1908, and 1910, hitting .260 in them. Harry died in 1914 in Bellevue, Kentucky.

Riggs Stephenson was called "Old Hoss." He came from Akron, Alabama, and batted and threw right-handed. He broke in with the Cleveland Indians in 1921, came over to the Cubs in 1926, and stayed there through 1934. He was known as one of the greatest clutch hitters of his time. He had a lifetime batting average of .336 and 63 homeruns. He led the league in doubles in 1927. Riggs was in two World Series with the Cubs, 1929 and 1932. He had 14 hits in 37 trips to the plate for a .378 batting average. Riggs died in Tuscaloosa, Alabama, in 1985.

Bobby Sturgeon came up to the Chicago Cubs in 1940 at the end of the season, playing in seven games. In 1941 he was the regular shortstop. In 1942 he played in 63 ballgames. He went into the service, and in 1946 and 1947 he played shortstop and second base for the Cubs. In 1948 he was with the Boston Braves. His six-year career showed a lifetime batting average of .257 with only one homerun. Bobby was a native of Clinton, Indiana.

Billy Sunday was a left-handed batter, threw right-handed, and played in the outfield. He played with Chicago in the old National League from 1883 through 1887. In 1888 and 1889 he was with Pittsburgh and then in the latter part of the 1890's he was with the Philadelphia Phillies. He played eight years, had a lifetime batting average of .248, and hit 12 homeruns but was best known as an evangelist. Billy died in November of 1935 in Chicago, Illinois. He was a native of Ames, Iowa.

Rick Sutcliffe is a major league veteran of 13 years from Independence, Missouri. He bats left and throws right. Rick started out with the Dodgers in 1976. He won 17 games in 1979, went to Cleveland in 1982, and won 14 games that year and 17 the next. In 1984 he came from Cleveland to the Cubs and won 20 games and lost six for the two ball clubs. He won 18 games in 1987 and 13 games in 1988. In 1989 he won 11, giving him a total of 128 wins against 103 losses in his 13 years in the big leagues. He was in the Championship Series in 1984, winning one game and losing one. In 1989 he was in the Championship Series again; he pitched six innings and was neither credited with a win nor charged with a loss.

Bruce Sutter was a right-handed pitcher from Lancaster, Pennsylvania. He started off with the Cubs in 1976 and pitched for them for five years. He went to the St. Louis Cardinals for four years and then to the Atlanta Braves. In 12 years he won 67 and lost 67. He was in 661 ballgames and never started a game; he was always used in relief. Bruce had a total of 300 saves lifetime. He was in the World Series in 1982 with St. Louis and was the winner in one game. He was not charged with any defeats.

A left-handed batter who also threw left-handed, **Chuck Tanner** came into the big leagues in 1955 with the Milwaukee Braves. In 1957 he came to the Cubs and remained with them through 1958. In 1959 and 1960 he was with Cleveland and he finished his eight-year career with the Dodgers in 1961 and 1962. In his eight years he had a lifetime batting average of .261 and hit 21 homeruns. Chuck managed the White Sox from 1970 through 1975; then he managed Oakland in 1976 and Pittsburgh from 1977 through 1985. He was the skipper at Atlanta in 1986 and 1987. He was the manager of the World Champion Pittsburgh Pirates in 1979 when they beat the Baltimore Orioles in seven games.

Joe Tinker was the shortstop in the Chicago Cubs famous Tinker-to-Evers-to-Chance double play combination. He was a scrappy, fearless performer and was an excellent hitter in the clutch. He came up with Chicago in 1902 and played there through 1912. He went to the Cincinnati Reds and then to the Chicago club in the Federal League in 1914 and 1915. He played his last season with the Chicago Cubs in 1916. In 15 years he had a .263 batting average. He managed the Reds in 1913, Chicago in the Federal League in 1914 and 1915, and the Cubs in 1916. He was admitted to baseball's Hall of Fame in 1946 and died in July of 1948.

Steve Trout had the great nickname of "Rainbow." He was the son of "Dizzy" Trout, who pitched for many years for the Detroit Tigers. Steve started his major league career in 1978 with the White Sox and came to the Cubs in 1983 along with Warren Brusstar, in exchange for Scott Fletcher, Randy Martz, Pat Tabler, and Dick Tidros. "Rainbow" stayed with the Cubs until 1987 when he went to the Yankees and later went to Seattle.

Johnny VanderMeer was called the "Dutch Master." He was a left-handed pitcher who twirled mainly for the Cincinnati Reds. He was with the Reds for 11 years, came to the Cubs in 1950, and finished his career in 1951 with Cleveland. Johnny became immortal in 1938 when he pitched two no-hit games in consecutive starts. His best year was in 1942 when he won 18 and lost 12, but he will be best remembered for the two no-hitters. He won 119 games and lost 121 in his 13 years. In 1938 he was with Cincinnati in the World Series. He was in one game and had no decision. With the Cubs in 1950 he won three and lost two.

Bill Veeck was a promotional genius! He started out as a stock-boy for the Chicago Cubs and worked his way to club treasurer. He joined Charlie Grimm in buying the Milwaukee Braves, a minor league team, and with many promotions built the attendance there. He lost a leg in the war and in 1947 headed a syndicate that bought the Cleveland Indians. He doubled the attendance there and won the World Series in 1948. He broke the color barrier, signing Larry Doby. He sold the Indians in 1949 and two years later bought the St. Louis Browns. He later bought the Chicago White Sox with Hank Greenberg and the Sox captured the pennant in 1959. Health forced him to retire in 1961 but he emerged again in 1975 to head a group to again buy the Sox. He sold the team in 1980. He is best remembered for sending a midget to the plate in St. Louis in 1951. He was a friend to everyone and spent his last few years watching games from the bleachers at Wrigley Field. He died on January 2, 1986 in Chicago, Illinois.

Rube Waddell, a left-handed pitcher who started his career off with Louisville in the old National League, went to Pittsburgh and then to Chicago in the National League. He was with the Philadelphia Athletics from 1902 through 1907 and finished his 13-year career with the St. Louis Browns in 1910. He was with the Chicago club in part of 1901, winning 13 games and losing 15. He won 191 games and lost 145 during his career. He was considered by many, including Connie Mack, as the greatest left-hander ever. Eccentric and colorful, he died in San Antonio, Texas, in April of 1914. He entered baseball's Hall of Fame in 1946.

Eddie Waitkus came from Cambridge, Massachusetts. He was a left-handed hitting first baseman who also threw left-handed. He came to the Cubs in 1941, went into the service, and came back after the war in 1946. He played three more years and went to the Phillies in 1949, where he stayed through 1953 when he went to Baltimore. He left Baltimore in the 1955 season and went back to the Phillies. His 11-year career showed a lifetime batting average of .285 with 24 homeruns. In the 1950 World Series he went to bat 15 times and got four hits for a .267 average. In 1949 when the Phillies

171

were visiting the Cubs and staying at the old Edgewater Beach Hotel, a girl named Ruth Steinhagen sent a note to Waitkus saying that she must see him immediately. When he knocked on her door, she invited him to come in and immediately shot him. There was no reason for the shooting, other than the girl's mental instability. Eddie recovered from this wound. He passed away in 1972 at Jamaica Plain, Massachusetts.

Jerome Walton started out in 1986 and played with Wytheville and then Peoria and Pittsfield. His first year in the major leagues was 1989 when he hit .293 with five homeruns. Jerome is a native of Newnan, Georgia. He won the batting championship when he played with Pittsfield in the Eastern League. He was the first Pittsfield player to win the title since 1976. In a poll of the Eastern League managers, he was ranked as the league's best defensive outfielder. He threw out three runners at homeplate on July 27 against Redding. In three minor league seasons Jerome had a .324 batting average and 112 stolen bases. He was the Cubs' second round draft choice in the 1986 January draft.

Lon Warneke was called "the Arkansas Hummingbird." He was a right-handed pitcher from Mt. Ida, Arkansas, and he was a dandy. He pitched for the Cubs from 1930 through 1936, three times winning 20 or more games. He won 22 and lost six in 1932 for a .786 percentage, the highest in the National League. He went to the Cardinals after the 1936 season in a trade for Rip Collins and Roy Parmelee. He had five excellent years with the Cardinals and came back with the Cubs in 1942. His 15 years in the big show gave him 193 victories and 121 defeats. In the World Series of 1932 he pitched in two games and was charged with one loss. In 1935 he pitched in three games and was credited with two wins and charged with no losses. He died in June of 1976 in Hot Springs, Arkansas.

Mitch Webster is a switch hitter from Larned, Kansas. He came to the Cubs from Montreal in exchange for Dave Martinez on July 14, 1988. His seven-year batting average is .273 with 43 homeruns. In the playoffs of 1989 he went to bat three times and got one hit.

Mitch started his major league career with Toronto in 1983 and went to Montreal in 1985. He was traded to Cleveland for Dane Clark in November of 1989.

Billy Williams joined the Cubs in 1959 and stayed with them through 1974. In 1975 and 1976 he was with the Oakland A's. His 18-year career showed a batting average of .290 and 426 homeruns. Billy was an outfielder and was the Cubs' perennial super batman. Winner of the National League Batting Championship in 1972, he was only the third Cub to win the title in all of baseball history. He was named Major League Player of the Year by the *Sporting News*, finished second in the Most Valuable Player balloting, and was elected Chicago Player of the Year by the Chicago Baseball Writers in 1972. He began his remarkable career in the big leagues in 1961 by being named Rookie of the Year in the National League. He was elected to baseball's Hall of Fame in 1989.

Fred Williams was much better known as "Cy." He came from Wadena, Indiana, and played with the Cubs from 1912 through 1917, when he went to the Phillies. He stayed with the Phillies through 1930. Fred was a powerful homerun hitter. He had a .292 lifetime batting average for his 19 years in the majors, and he had 251 homeruns. Four times he led the National League in homeruns: 1916, when he was with the Cubs; and 1920, 1923, and 1927, when he was with the Phillies. Cy never played in a World Series. He died in Eagle River, Wisconsin, in April of 1974.

Mitch Williams is a left-handed pitcher who came from Santa Ana, California. He joined the major leagues with Texas in 1986. He pitched there for three years and came over to the Cubs in 1989. He was the winning pitcher in four games and lost four times. An extremely colorful pitcher, he was credited with a save in 36 games. His record now is 22 wins and 23 defeats, and he has 68 saves in his four years in the majors.

Hack Wilson compiled a .307 batting average over 12 major league seasons, but he was mainly a power hitter. He started his career with the Giants in 1923, came to the Cubs in 1926, went to Brooklyn in 1932, and joined the Phillies in 1934. In 1930 he had 190 runs batted in, which is still the all-time major league record, and he had 56 homeruns, which is a National League record. Hack passed away in November of 1948, in Baltimore, Maryland. Four times he led the league in homeruns and twice in RBI's. He was admitted to baseball's Hall of Fame in 1979. He hit 244 homers in his career and died in Baltimore, Maryland, in 1948.

Don Zimmer, a right-handed batter who threw right-handed, is now the manager of the Cubs. He started his major league career in 1954 with the Dodgers, came to the Cubs in 1960, went to the Mets in 1962, and then moved on to Cincinnati. In 1963 he was with the Dodgers and then the Washington Senators. He wound up his 12-year career in the major leagues in 1965 with Washington. He had a .235 lifetime batting average and a total of 91 homeruns. He was mainly a third baseman, but he played some short and second base. He also caught in 35 games. Don was in the 1955 World Series with Brooklyn and the 1959 World Series with Los Angeles. He went to bat 10 times in the two series and got two hits for a .200 average. Don managed the San Diego Padres in 1972 and 1973. He managed the Boston Red Sox from 1976 through 1980 and in 1981 and 1982 he managed the Texas ball club. He piloted the Cubs in 1988 and 1989 and was named National League Manager of the Year in 1989.

Heine Zimmerman played 13 years in the National League. He started with the Cubs in 1907 and in 1916 went to the Giants. He hit .295 lifetime with 58 homers. Heine played in three World Series, with the Cubs in 1907 and 1910, and with the Giants in 1917. He went to bat 43 times and got seven hits for a .163 average. In a run down play in the sixth game of the 1917 World Series, Zimmerman chased Eddie Collins over the plate with a run. He was hardly to blame because the catcher, Bill Rariden, and first baseman, Walter Holke, had left the home station uncovered. He died in March of 1969, in New York City.